Ohashi was born near Hiroshima, Japan, in 1944. He was a sickly child, but his strength was restored by ancient Japanese healing techniques. Because he owed his life to the Eastern concept of health, he later dedicated himself to teaching it to others. After graduating from Chuo University in Tokyo, Ohashi studied Eastern healing arts with many masters. In 1970 he settled in the United States and established the Ohashi Institute, a nonprofit educational organization located in New York City. He and his Certified Ohashiatsu® Instructors teach his own system of technique, exercise, and mediation in many cities in Europe and the United States.

Tom Monte is the former editor of *Nutrition Action* and former associate editor of *East West Journal*. His numerous books on health and environmental issues include *Recalled by Life: The Story of My Recovery from Cancer*, written with Dr. Andrew Sattilaro; *The Way of Hope*; and *Pritikin: The Man Who Healed America's Heart*, written by Ilene Pritikin, widow of Dr. Nathan Pritikin. His work has appeared in numerous magazines and newspapers in Europe and the United States.

READING THE BODY

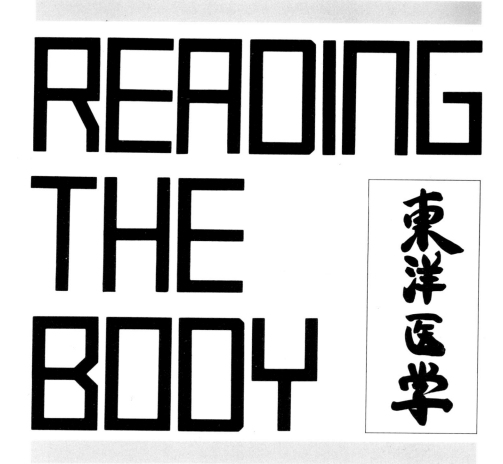

Ohashi's Book of
Oriental Diagnosis

Ohashi
with Tom Monte

Aquarian/Thorsons
An Imprint of HarperCollins*Publishers*

The Aquarian Press
An Imprint of HarperCollins*Publishers*
77–85 Fulham Palace Road,
Hammersmith, London W6 8JB

Published by the Aquarian Press 1992
First published in the USA in 1991 by Arkana Books,
part of Viking Penguin, 375 Hudson Street, New York, NY 10014
10 9 8 7 6 5 4 3 2 1

© Wataru Ohashi and Tom Monte 1991
Illustrations © Peter Sinclair 1991
Calligraphy by Ohashi

Wataru Ohashi and Tom Monte assert the moral right
to be identified as the authors of this work

A catalogue record for this book
is available from the British Library

ISBN 1 85538 213 8

Printed in Great Britain by
Woolnough Bookbinding Limited,Irthlingborough

A NOTE THE THE READER
The ideas, procedures and suggestions contained in this book
are not intended as a substitute for consulting with your
doctor. All matters regarding your health require medical
supervision

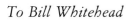

To Bill Whitehead

Preface

As I finish my fifth book I realize again how each book one writes has its own biography, just as each human has his or her own life story. Fifteen years ago I intended the material in *Oriental Diagnosis* to be part of my first book, *Do-It-Yourself Shiatsu*. My editor then, Bill Whitehead, felt that we should not include the section on Oriental diagnosis in that book, both because of space limitations and because he felt there was not yet sufficient interest in the subject. I did not agree, but accepted his decision, and *Do-It-Yourself Shiatsu*, published by E. P. Dutton, became a best-seller. Over the last fifteen years it has become something of a classic, and has been translated into seven languages.

After that book came out Mr. Whitehead encouraged me to write *Reading the Body* as a sequel. Even after he moved on to another publishing house we occasionally got together to discuss it, and he was kind enough to give me good suggestions. But I personally became very busy in my life—starting the Ohashi Institute, teaching and lecturing here in the States and in Europe, and marrying and raising a child— and did not write it. But I was working on it in my mind. I have given more than sixty lectures and workshops on Oriental diagnosis, teaching more than five thousand people in the United States and Europe about the subject. I received a tremendous amount of enthusiastic response and interest, always accompanied by many questions and requests for advice.

Many people besides my publisher have been impatient with me for not finishing this book sooner. I rewrote some of the material several times, because as I grow each year I find that what I used to believe is not necessarily what I believe now—I see more clearly what I thought I saw clearly before.

Over the years I have gained in knowledge and experience. The ideas contained in this book have fermented and matured, aided by the leaven of my interactions with hundreds of students and by my personal growth. These years have given aroma and flavor and richness to this book.

Kikuchi Kan, one of my favorite Japanese writers, wrote that we shouldn't write any book before age forty-five because we don't complete our philosophy until then. I respected his opinion when I was a college boy in Tokyo, but by now I have also experienced the truth in this statement. Now that I have reached the age of forty-five, it seems time to let this book be born, so it can live in the world on its own and interact with people. Books are like children, born from a parent. As they grow, moving through childhood and into adulthood, they influence the parent, who changes because of the child. At some point the parent has to acknowledge the independence of the child. I am very perplexed at this moment to finally let this book be published. On the one hand, I am pleased to have it exist. On the other hand, I'm scared and unhappy that it is not a perfect book because I am still growing and studying all the time, and expect to learn something new tomorrow.

Though I would like to write a perfect book, I can't. So I decided to make myself finish this book as best as I can in order to present it to you, and I am asking you to give me your responses, advice, and encouragement so that I may grow more and change in the next twenty years. I will be very happy to write another book on this subject when I reach sixty-five, though I expect I will feel the same frustrations then. I see that while each book has its own biography, the biography cannot be finished by the author. At least that's true of the kind of book I always respect and enjoy the most, and I hope this book is one of those.

Ohashi
June 1991

Acknowledgments

IN ORDER TO ACCOMPLISH SOMETHING IN our lives, we need not only hard work but also great luck. I have been blessed with both of them. I am very happy that in the last fifteen years I have had so much healthy energy, enthusiasm, and well-being. And I am blessed to have had much luck and the help of many people.

First of all, I want to express my sincere appreciation to Bill Whitehead, who published my first book at E. P. Dutton. He continually encouraged me to finish this book, and I consulted with him many times. I still remember a summer evening he shared with my family in Riverside Park, watching my small son play while we discussed the book.

It was ten years later that Paul De Angelis bought this book for E. P. Dutton, and he worked with me on the ideas of the book and on the manuscript. My family and his family became close to one another in the process, and on another summer evening we watched his small daughter play in the grass while we talked.

After E. P. Dutton became part of Penguin USA, and Paul De Angelis went to another house, I met David Stanford, the editor who gave me thoughtful consultation to refine the book to its finished form. He and I have not spent a summer evening together in a park, but toward the end of the editing process I was prisoner for several days in his office, reviewing the many miracles performed by Barbara Perris, an astute copyeditor. I want to express my happiness at having the good fortune to work with Tom Monte, who is my collaborator for this book. He has a tremendous amount of energy and knowledge, and sometimes forced me to speed up my lazy writing process with his high-tech computerization. He has great experience and knowledge of Oriental healing, including macrobiotics and bodywork, and without his collaboration and talent this book would never have been completed. He and I had a hard time concentrating on writing since both of us like to talk so much about human evolution, spirituality, ecology, and the destiny of mankind. He stayed at my home many days over the course of our writing this book, and we became close friends.

Peter Sinclair originally came to our school to study the Ohashiatsu® Program. When I discovered he had great talent as an artist, I convinced him to work on this book. He happily accepted my invitation to draw some of the illustrations and delivered them with great enthusiasm and spirit and contributed much to the book. He too spent many days with me in my house near Albany, New York. Since he and his family live in Michigan he sacrificed a good deal to come and work with me and I am deeply grateful. Meanwhile, he succeeded in graduating from the Ohashiatsu® Program, an accomplishment which I highly admire. I also want to extend appreciation to my students and to the instructors in my Institute who have been waiting for fifteen years for this book, and who politely smiled each time I promised that it would be out "in three months."

My sincere appreciation goes to you who are holding this book in your hands at this moment. I always try to see what I don't see, and I am looking forward to receiving your honest responses to this book. I would also be very happy to come and give my workshop and lecture and to share my happiness and experience with you. Please write to me:

Ohashi
P.O. Box 505
Kinderhook, NY 12106
U.S.A.

Contents

Reading the Body

1

What Is
Oriental Diagnosis?

LONG BEFORE THERE WERE X-RAY MACHINES, CAT scans, and blood tests, traditional healers used noninvasive methods to ascertain personal health, talents, and character. From their understanding came a deep appreciation for the unity of the mind, body, and spirit. For the Oriental diagnostician, the body is the physical manifestation of the soul. Body and soul are one. The body is both a symptom and a symbol of the spirit.

Oriental diagnosis is the art of seeing beneath the superficial to the profound; of revealing the inner truth. In this book, I will talk not only about your health, but also about your inner nature as it is revealed in the physical characteristics of your body. I will help you gain insight into your true nature. You will look beyond old prejudices, guilt, and misconceptions to see a deeper, more fundamental you.

All people are searching for answers to life's most important questions: Who am I? What are my strengths? What are my weaknesses? What is my direction in life? I will teach you to read your body like a book in which are written the answers to these questions.

My goal is to show you your good points, the areas in which you are strong, evolved, and talented. I want you to know what is right about you! I want you to develop a deep appreciation for the person you are.

The more aware you become of your strengths, the more easily you can choose to go in the direction of your talents and happiness. Awareness improves the quality of your life.

I do not believe you must change to be happy. Rather, you must know and cultivate what is good about you. You already possess all you need to be happy.

We have many misconceptions about ourselves. Most people today think there is something wrong with them. They think they have to change to be happy. This attitude encourages them to feel inferior and guilty.

My way is different. Each of us is already good enough; we are already capable of being happy. The key is to know and cultivate the good within.

As we come to know ourselves, we begin to see both our strengths and our weaknesses. Through Oriental diagnosis, we see our weaknesses in their true light: as guidelines for behavior, not as something to feel bad about.

For example, let's say that your intestines are weak. Rather than using this knowledge to criticize yourself, you can use it to make yourself happy by treating your intestines gently and with respect. Through self-knowledge, you can choose your foods carefully; you can choose to chew well and to eat in a calm, peaceful way. Gradually, your intestines grow stronger and stronger; you think more clearly and develop much more confidence. Now you use your self-knowledge to make yourself happy, rather than to promote self-criticism and misery.

Specifically, you will learn two things from this book. The first is a new way of seeing yourself and others based on the ancient methods of Oriental diagnosis. You will come to recognize that every characteristic, every gesture, every line on your face has meaning. You will come to know the specific meaning of each of these characteristics, gestures, and lines. Through this process, you will realize a fundamental truth about life: that the answers to all its important questions already exist within you.

My students always ask me, "Ohashi, where should I go to find enlightenment? Should I go to Japan or India? Should I study with this guru or that one?" Or they ask, "What should I do to improve my health?" or "What should I do for a living?" People are always going somewhere or to someone else looking for answers to these questions. Many people pay huge sums of money to have someone tell them about themselves, or to help them figure out who they are, but the more money they spend the more confused and disappointed they become.

The answers do not exist outside of us. They are inside. The response I give my students is very simple, yet it is the gateway to all answers. "You are standing on your answer," I tell them. "The answer is you." What I mean is that the answers already exist within you. The real question is how to find them.

You do not have to go to this specialist or that one. You do not have to listen endlessly to self-help lectures. All you have to do is learn to read your own book—the words of which are written on the features of your body.

Before entering my classroom, I ask my students to take off their shoes. It is a Japanese tradition not to wear shoes indoors. Often I pick out several pairs of shoes from my students and, without asking who they belong to, I read the bottoms of their shoes for the stories of their inner natures. "I see that this person has lower-back ache," I say. Inevitably, someone will let out an embarrassed giggle—the guilty party, no doubt. "Oh, but you have wonderful intestines, strong will, and a positive outlook on life," I go on. "Keep it up. With this, you will succeed." I add, "Be careful to treat your kidneys well. There is a little weakness there." I then move to the next pair of shoes and make another round of observations. "A very stubborn person walks in these shoes," I say with mock gravity. "We must give him good Ohashiatsu* to loosen him up." The class laughs. "The stubbornness comes from a weak spleen," I continue. "He is very determined, but very frustrated. He must learn to see the good things in himself and the great things he has accomplished already."

On and on I go. People marvel at this. They think it's a magic show, but it is nothing more than knowledge.

Oriental diagnosis will help you see beneath the surface of things to your inner being. But to see the inner you, you must practice seeing the good in yourself and in others. Oriental diagnosis is a guide to a positive and happy life. But you must develop the ability to be positive. This is the power in life that endures, builds, and eventually succeeds.

The second thing you will learn from this book is to cultivate your simple common sense. Out of this will come a natural, broader way of thinking. Your mind will go beyond the duality of good and bad. You will develop a more holistic view of life. You will see that within all things lie opposites. You are not a weak person or a strong person— you are both at once!

Here is a fundamental difference between Orientals and Westerners. Westerners see things in absolutes: something is either good or bad, right or wrong, strong or weak.

In the Orient, we see everything as both strong and weak at the same time. A tree that bends easily can be seen as weak. But that same tree has the power to give way to a powerful wind. Therefore, it survives when others break. The tree's flexibility is its strength.

Let me give you another example. From a Western medical perspective, a person who has symptoms of disease is seen as sick. This defines the person and his or her treatment.

But the traditional Oriental healer sees within the sick person a struggle taking place between sickness and health. If no health were

* Ohashiatsu is the form of bodywork developed by Ohashi based on his study of shiatsu, acupuncture, mexabution, manipulation, ken do, aikido, and dance, as well as Oriental philosophy.

present, the patient would be dead. Becoming sick is a sign of health. As long as you are sick, you are alive. As long as you are alive, you have a chance to recover. When you are dead, you have no more chances.

So the Oriental healer's approach is to encourage the forces of health within the patient. As a result, our methods of healing are very different from those used in the West. You will see this more clearly—and understand our reasoning—as I explain ways of dealing with various health problems.

Several years ago, a husband and wife came to me for advice. The man had been to many doctors already and was suffering from more than thirty ailments. His wife said to me, "Ohashi, don't you think my husband is very sick?"

I stood up and put my hands on the man's shoulders in admiration. I said, "I have never met such a healthy man in all my life. If I had one of these problems, I would be kaputo—dead! But you have thirty of them, and you are still walking around. You are alive. You must possess so much strength within you. You must be so healthy, too."

The man was so grateful for my words that he almost cried. Everyone stigmatized him as a sick man. No one gave him any hope of recovery. I gave him hope, and it was true: he did get well.

In the Orient, we never see anything as one way or the other. We see everything as having opposites within. Paradox exists in everything.

If you only see the bad in someone or something, you only see half the picture. In that sense, you are blind to the possibilities within the person or the situation. There is little or no hope anymore, because there is no reason for hope. Consequently, you cannot help suffering. But if you open up to the good that is also there, you will have a whole new view of life, and you will enjoy yourself and your life greatly.

I am not saying that East is better than West. I believe both are essential to the whole. The medical practices of the West have done wonderful and miraculous things for us. But just as important are the philosophy and approach of the Orient, whose methods are often more gentle, more interested in the cause of the problems, and just as effective as those used by the Western medical doctor. The important point is that both have their place in the spectrum of healing. East and West are opposites, complementing each other, making the world possible.

In this book, I will concentrate on the methods used in traditional Oriental healing. To help you understand Oriental diagnosis and its underlying philosophy, I will sometimes contrast the ways of East and West. But as you come to understand my approach, you will see that both sides have value. Whether you choose one or the other at any particular moment depends on the situation you face and what you are trying to accomplish.

HOW TO USE THIS BOOK

Each of us—no matter who we are, no matter how much we already know—must approach the discipline of Oriental diagnosis in the same way: as a student. I have been studying Oriental diagnosis for the past twenty-five years, and I will continue as a student for the rest of my life. My attitude as a beginner ensures that I will always learn. In the process, I hope I will develop my understanding of life itself. That is the purpose of this practice.

The pursuit of self-knowlege is a lifelong endeavor. Whenever I look in the mirror or examine my face, I am confronted with some new information. Today I am clear and bright; tomorrow I may be dull and dark. I ask myself, What is my body telling me today? How should I adjust to my changing condition? I am always the student of change.

When I look at other people's faces, I see their changing conditions and learn from their faces and postures, the ways in which they walk, talk, and gesture. I marvel at the infinite creativity of the universe and at the same time recognize the similarity of the patterns.

As long as we are alive, we are learning. Therefore, we are always students. Oriental diagnosis is our tool for discovering life's wisdom.

Your ability as an Oriental diagnostician depends solely on your personal development as a human being. If you think you know something already, you are less likely to remain open to a greater truth or deeper insight. You are too cluttered with self-importance and limited ideas. But if you are always a student, you will constantly be expanding your understanding and abilities. Life will constantly surprise you with new insight and knowledge. As your wisdom grows, you will look with fresh eyes on your own face and the faces of others. You will see ever more clearly that each of us is a unique manifestation of the infinite universe. Always remember, the more you can love and understand people, the more they will reveal themselves to you, and the greater service you can provide them.

No matter what your reasons for reading this book, approach it as a student. Be a beginner, and you will benefit greatly from this book, and from all of life.

Besides seeing yourself as a beginner, another essential when reading this book is to free yourself of all ethnic or racial bias.

Every ethnic group has physical traits that make it unique. Japanese, Chinese, and other Oriental people have distinct, characteristic eyes, yellow skin, and black hair. They are generally shorter than Westerners, too. Many Eastern Europeans have large noses and curly hair. Many Swedes have light skin and hair. Africans have black skin, dark eyes, and curly hair; many have large lips. Southern Italians have dark skin and hair; many have large, so-called Roman noses. Arabs have dark skin, hair, and eyes; many have wide mouths with larger lips. American Indians have wide faces, high cheekbones, and dark skin; many have straight hair.

The point is, every ethnic and racial group has its own unique physical features; when examining the face of a particular person, you must see that person within his or her own ethnic grouping to understand the information coming from the person's face. For example, as you will learn later in this book, the bottom lip indicates the condition of the large intestine. To know whether a person's lip is swollen or tight, you must see it in relationship to the person's mouth and face. Moreover, you cannot compare the lips of an African-American to those of a German-American, for example, or the nose of a Japanese to that of a Sicilian, if you want an accurate understanding of the person's health.

Beyond this practical reason for freeing oneself from prejudice, it's also true that those who maintain racial or ethnic prejudice have an extremely limited understanding of life. When we use Oriental diagnosis, we are trying to understand how the infinite manifests in the finite, how each of us is a unique manifestation of the divine. Perhaps if you have the opportunity to study the endless variations of the human face and body through Oriental diagnosis, as I have, you will gain a heightened understanding of the beauty of each and every person.

ORIENTAL DIAGNOSIS: FOUR FUNDAMENTAL TRUTHS

Let's begin with the four basic ideas of Oriental diagnosis.

All phenomena are composed of opposites. Paradox is present in everything. No matter where you look in nature, you will see the interplay of opposites. Without paradox, there would be no physical world. For example, a single day is composed of light and dark; the human race is composed of man and woman; there would be no "hot" if there were no "cold." The brain has left and right hemispheres, each performing complementary functions. All things have left and right, front and back, high and low. Without opposites, there would be no way to distinguish anything on the planet. Life would have no form.

In the Orient, we say that one extreme gives rise to its opposite. A poor man has the capacity to become rich, a sick person can become healthy; a healthy person can become sick, a rich man poor. The more extreme your condition, the greater your chance of achieving its opposite. Every problem can be turned into an advantage.

What I am saying is this: no matter how bad your situation may appear to be, a tremendous possibility exists for growth and happiness. All you need to do is find the good and develop it. This attitude alone is your answer. Your attitude toward reality can form the basis for positive change. Fact is fact; yes, you have a problem. The question is: How will you respond to it? Will you give up because you think the problem is too much for you, or will you look at your problem as your opportunity? How you look at your problem determines how you deal with it. Your attitude is in your power. Change your attitude and you can see your problem in a different light.

Let me give you an example. When I came to this country, I had many difficulties. One night, I became very depressed. I sat by myself in a quiet room and cried and cried. After I finished crying, I made a list of my troubles. They seemed overwhelming. This was my list:

1. I am Japanese. It is good to be Japanese if you are in Japan, but it is hard to be Japanese in America. There is much to adjust to in a foreign land, and I have many difficulties dealing with the customs, culture, and expectations of America.
2. I do not speak good English. I can barely understand what people are saying in English.
3. I have no money. And since I do not speak English well, how can I get a good job?
4. I have no friends or family. I am alone. Whom can I turn to for help? No one.

These were my central problems, but of course they caused many other difficulties and frustrations in the course of a day.

After I had made my list, I sat to meditate. After my meditation I examined the list I had made. Suddenly I realized that the things I had seen as my troubles were actually my opportunities! One by one, I went down my list:

1. I am Japanese. Great! I will make the most of being Japanese. I can teach Oriental diagnosis and Ohashiatsu to the Americans. Because I happen to be short and nearsighted and have slanted eyes, people will see me as authentic. I will get more respect for my work.
2. I do not speak good English. Great! I don't have to listen when people complain about me. My mind will be peaceful.
3. I have no money. Terrific! Then even a quarter will be more than I had before. I have nowhere to go but up. I am already on my way to success.
4. I have no friends or family. Fantastic! I am not a prisoner of their advice or expectations. I am not restricted by the bonds of family or social structure. I am free.

As soon as I stopped thinking of these situations as my problems, I was able to go on with my life and become freer and content. I saw these problems in their true light: as my opportunities! Fact was still fact. Nothing had changed except my point of view, which gave me more freedom to improve my life.

My situation did improve. When I started to teach Oriental diagnosis and Ohashiatsu in New York City, I had only a few students. But very rapidly, things changed, and today I have two thousand students and many schools throughout the United States and Europe. The Ohashi Institute is well recognized around the world.

Problems are the seeds of good fortune. They provide insight into who we truly are. They also make us appreciate benefits. Everyone has good within, special abilities or talents. We must have the courage to exploit our abilities and talents if we are to have any chance at succeeding in life.

The idea of paradox is not limited to the Orient. The Greek philosopher Heraclitus built his entire philosophy on it. "Opposition brings accord," wrote Heraclitus. "Out of discord comes the fairest harmony. . . . It is by disease that health is pleasant, by evil that good is pleasant, by hunger satiety, by weariness rest."

Problems are the mother of growth and success. Embrace your problems and you will find your answers.

Once one of my students came to me and said he felt hopeless. He had so many troubles. I said, "You are right, you are hopeless."

He was shocked that I said this. But then I explained: "We are all hopeless. But this realization can make you happy. If you truly believe you are hopeless, then everything you accomplish is a bonanza! You were hopeless and yet you accomplished all of this? You are amazing." I stood up and shook his hand. "Congratulations; you are an amazing young fellow."

This is my philosophy: appreciation is the key to happiness. If you consider yourself hopeless, you will truly appreciate everything you do, everything you accomplish, and everything that is given to you. Failure will not be so painful. After all, you were doomed to begin with.

I was born in 1944 in a small town outside Hiroshima. By the age of three, I had had three opportunities to die. The first came in 1945, when my town was bombed with conventional explosives and then the atomic bomb was dropped on Hiroshima. Fortunately, my family lived beyond the atomic blast site, but the effects of the conventional bombing on my hometown were devastating. I suffered terrible diarrhea, dehydration, and other side effects of poor sanitation. A local doctor had to work very hard to keep me alive. But I lived. Within two years, I suffered two accidents, either of which could have killed me. But I lived.

In 1991, I turned forty-seven years of age. I am so excited to be alive. I have lived forty-four years longer than expected. Even if I die tomorrow, no one can say Ohashi died young. Ohashi has already lived longer than he could have expected. Every day is a fringe benefit.

You see, the true pleasure of life comes from simplicity, but we cannot appreciate simple joys because we expect too much. When we expect too much, we are unable to appreciate anything—even ourselves.

Embrace your weaknesses, recognize how limited your chances of success have been, and then appreciate everything. You have done a wonderful job.

The principle of opposites is ancient. It formed the basis of the first medical book ever written, *The Yellow Emperor's Classic of Internal Medicine,* a great Chinese work that provides the foundation for all Oriental medicine. *The Yellow Emperor's Classic* articulates the philosophy of opposites as *yin* and *yang,* the two forces that make all phenomena possible. Yin is described as the expansive force in the universe. It causes centrifugal force; it makes things tall, wet, loose, and feminine. Yang is described as the contractive force, causing centripetality; it makes things small, dry, tight, and masculine. These two primordial forces are viewed as archetypes in the Orient, that is, the two essential forces that bring about all events in the physical world.

I will discuss yin and yang in greater depth later, pointing out yin characteristics and yang characteristics in our bodies and patterns of behavior. I will also consider yin and yang in the Oriental approach to correcting various imbalances in our bodies.

Each human being is a unified whole of body, mind, and spirit. There is no separation among these human characteristics. The body could not exist without the mind and soul; neither could the mind or spirit exist on earth without the body. The three aspects of human life are one. No problem can be solved without dealing with all three realms.

When I discuss Oriental diagnosis, I often say that a symptom indicates physical, psychological, and spiritual characteristics. The reason is that the physical is a symptom of the mental and spiritual. It is by the spirit that we came to be.

The whole can be seen in any one of the parts. In the micro we can see the macro, and in the macro we can see the micro. This means that in any single part of the body we can see the workings of the whole. By examining the face, we can see the condition of the digestive, circulatory, and nervous systems; the heart; the sex organs; the kidneys; the liver and gallbladder; and the spleen. In addition, we can see many personal characteristics, including talents, tendencies, strengths, and weaknesses. The face reveals the secrets of the body and spirit.

• • •

Energy flows throughout the body in exquisitely organized patterns, or channels, called meridians. These meridians are rivers of energy that run from head to foot, creating an interconnected web that links every cell and organ with every other part of the body. Later in this book you will see how these meridians can be examined to reveal the health of individual organs.

The unity of life is awesome. Virtually every major religion and philosophy throughout time has pointed to this unity; it is the most basic of all tenets. "Hear O Israel, the Lord our God, the Lord is One" is but one expression of this fundamental principle. Oriental diagnosis, which is also based on this principle of unity, is therefore not only a technique or tool, but also a philosophical and religious path. It leads us into the mainspring of life, which is divinity within. It should be approached with an attitude of humility, reverence, and appreciation. Never use it as a tool to criticize yourself or others. Never allow it to become a means of enforcing inferiority or weakness on yourself or others. It is meant to uplift and inspire. It is meant to guide us to the oneness.

DIAGNOSIS: EAST AND WEST

I must admit that the word "diagnosis" is a bit misleading. I am not diagnosing as a medical doctor does. In fact, there are so many differences between Western medicine and Oriental diagnosis that contrasting them can help you better understand the Oriental approach. (See Chart 1.)

Let's begin with the broadest differences. In the Orient, the human body is viewed as a finely balanced unity of interdependent parts. More important, the whole is greater than the sum of its parts.

You are a living entity that is composed of mind, body, and spirit. An Oriental diagnostician views all three realms as one. There is no separation, only unity.

In Oriental diagnosis, we see the body as an orchestra whose music is the soul. Remove any instrument, or change the way it is played, and you alter the music entirely. To bring out the full breadth of the spirit, you must finely tune each organ as if it were an instrument. It must function optimally, as if it were being played by a virtuoso. Yet you must never forget that each organ must blend harmoniously with the rest of the body—all the other pieces of the orchestra—to bring forth the most complete and beautiful being, which is you.

The Oriental healer, therefore, is like the conductor of an orchestra.

He or she hears the instruments that are playing out of tune and adjusts them to bring each into harmony with the rest of the orchestra.

Let's investigate more closely now.

Within the body, each organ is seen in relation to all the others. The health of an individual organ—the liver, for example—depends on the healthy functioning of every other organ. The reason is simple: from the Oriental point of view, the body is a continuous circuit in which energy flows. This energy is the life force. In Japan it is called *ki;* in China it is referred to as *chi;* in India it is called *prana.* If the energy is blocked in any part of the body, other organs fail to be nourished adequately with energy, or ki.

Thus, the liver, heart, spleen, large intestine, and kidneys—to name just a few—are all working in harmony, each one dependent on the others for health. If there is an adequate flow of ki throughout the body, every cell will be nourished with life-giving energy. Every organ will be able to perform its tasks optimally. If the energy is blocked, cells and organs suffocate from a lack of ki.

The same words can have different meanings in Western and Eastern diagnosis. In the Western tradition if we speak of "the liver" or "problems of the liver" we are speaking only of physical problems of the organ itself. In the Eastern tradition we could be speaking of the organ itself or of the energy meridian that relates to that organ, and problems affecting that organ or meridian are sometimes physical and sometimes psychological.

To speak of the body as separate from the life energy, or spirit, is misleading. Your body is the outward manifestation of your spirit. The spirit, or life force, imbues the body and maintains its life. The Oriental healer works with the body's energy. We are concerned with the characteristics and behavior of each organ. Is it too tight, for example, causing energy to be trapped there? Is this the cause of the pain or degeneration? Or is the organ swollen? Is adequate energy flowing to that part of the body? I ask myself, What in the life-style, diet, or behavior is causing the imbalance? These are only a few of the questions we will be asking as we look more closely at our bodies later in the book.

Because the mind, spirit, and body are one, every human characteristic—whether emotional, intellectual, or spiritual—has a corresponding physical organ. We all know, for example, that the brain is the organ for thinking, yet no scientist or brain surgeon has ever seen a thought. Thoughts are invisible, but if the brain is injured our capacity to think is diminished. It is the same elsewhere in the body. Each organ has a role in maintaining the character of the person.

In Oriental diagnosis, we say that the health of the body is directly related to the health of the mind and to personal psychology. We even say that each emotion is associated with a particular organ or group of

CHART 1 DIAGNOSIS: EAST AND WEST

Oriental	Western
Abstract	Concrete/specific
Subjective	Objective
Artistic	Technical/scientific
Right brain	Left brain
Oriental medicine developed from philosophy and art	Western medicine developed from science
Oriental medicine meant to develop a person spiritually; concerned with how well one understands	Western medicine more materialistically concerned; physical symptoms emphasized
Oriental diagnosis imprecise; very general	Western medicine very precise; concerned with what's wrong
Holistic; concerned with whole person, not specific complaint	Symptomatic; focused on specific organs, symptoms, rather than the workings of whole person
Based on human-to-human communication; touching	Based on machines and laboratory tests
Oriental medicine based on paradox: health based on balance between opposites, or opposing (paradoxical) forces— "Sickness suggests health; health suggests sickness"	Western medicine linear: "Health is health; sickness is sickness"—good and bad are pure and separate
Sickness suggests strength to eliminate; problem can be turned to advantage	
Everything changes	Conditions seen as static
Accepts difficulties and death	Does not accept difficulties or death; does everything possible to avoid both
Medicine is general, life-style–oriented	Medicine is precise, drug- and surgery-oriented
Patient heals himself; healer only guides	Doctor and medicine heal patient
Healer more passive	Doctor more paternal, aggressive
Healer and patient involved in relationship in which both give and both receive, healer grateful to patient—giver is receiver, and receiver is giver	Doctor gives medicine, patient not seen as giving anything— doctor is giver and patient is receiver

organs. (I will discuss this at length in the chapters that follow.) The liver, for example, is related to anger. When the liver is troubled or injured, you have more anger in your life. The kidneys are the seat of the will and control fear. The more troubled the kidneys, the more fear you experience. (Again, we will look at each organ and its corresponding emotional and psychological aspects later.)

In Oriental diagnosis, then, we do not think of taking out a gallbladder or spleen without recognizing that the whole person will be changed, will cease to be who he or she was. Instead of performing surgery, the healer attempts to rectify the underlying problem by dealing with its essential cause.

This philosophy emerges from the Oriental way of thinking, which is dominated by the right hemisphere of the brain. The Oriental mind thinks in a holistic and intuitive fashion, as opposed to a segmentalized and rational one. Oriental philosophy is humanistic and artistic, rather than technological. For the Oriental, life is a picture in which all the elements are essential to the whole. Remove any single element and you have altered the picture entirely, creating a new scene.

Oriental diagnosis depends entirely on human-to-human contact. The Oriental practitioner observes his or her patient, touches the patient, questions him or her closely, and listens carefully.

The relationship between patient and healer is so close as to be one. The healer must let go of ego and let observations, intuition, and the information coming from the patient direct his or her actions. The Oriental healer's role is passive and nurturing.

In Oriental diagnosis, we try to work with the health-restoring energies inside the patient. The healer doesn't heal; the patient heals. All the healer does is guide the patient to help himself or herself recover. Thus, the healer is essentially humble.

Oriental healing takes the long view. We look at the big picture, the whole person. We emphasize prevention of disease. We seek to maintain and enhance health.

In ancient China, a doctor was paid to maintain the good health of the patient. If the patient became sick, the doctor did not get paid. The court physician was beheaded when the king became ill. Prevention of disease was the primary "medicine."

Another difference between Eastern and Western medicine is that Oriental medicine emphasizes person-to-person contact. This is not a mass-market approach, but a slow, painstaking process in which we merge, as much as possible, with the unique life of another person.

Oriental diagnosis is like life; it is imprecise. I like to say that we Oriental practitioners are mushy, mushy. Our approach to the person is gentle and maternal. We assist the person in getting well. Our intention is to help the person use his or her own healing abilities.

Oriental diagnosis and healing is an art. More precisely, it is a spiritual practice. It is learning to foster the quality and art of life.

Western diagnosis is based on the Western approach to life, which is left-brained, analytical, technical, and scientific. The relationship between doctor and patient is de-emphasized in favor of laboratory reports, blood tests, and other tests.

Objectivity is stressed. Machines are used to examine, elicit facts, measure, and form a scientific diagnosis, rather than to direct human perception. These machines are wonderfully precise. The doctor attempts to be professionally detached from his or her patient. The doctor's personal observations, intuition, and emotions are secondary to the measurements of machines.

Because machines and tests are emphasized, doctors can see hundreds of patients. It is a mass-market approach. And there are no in-betweens; in the eyes of a medical doctor, either you are healthy or you are sick— one or the other, never both.

Western medicine defines sickness based on symptoms. Therefore, its approach to healing is symptomatic. For a headache, a doctor offers aspirin. Usually the doctor doesn't concern himself or herself with the underlying cause of the headache. Even when stress or diet is the obvious cause of the headache, the approach is the same: a drug. A skin rash is usually dealt with by using topical ointments; the underlying cause of the rash is not considered. Digestive problems are handled with Tums, Rolaids, Alka-Seltzer, or stronger medicines.

In the Oriental diagnostician's mind, a headache, skin rash, or digestive problem may be the result of kidney, liver, or spleen problems, any one of which might be caused by diet, stress, or psychological troubles. The Oriental approach would not be to prescribe a drug, but to suggest alterations in life-style.

The Western medical doctor takes the microscopic view, tending to look at the tiny world of bacteria, viruses, and other microscopic organisms. This further encourages the use of drugs. For the medical doctor, drugs are used until the problem becomes too big for drugs; then surgery is the answer. Tonsillitis is dealt with by the removal of the tonsils; gallbladder diseases often results in the removal of the gallbladder. Heart disease is treated by bypass or open-heart surgery. And so on. The two primary tools of modern medicine are drugs and surgery, which are used to treat symptoms.

The underlying reason for this symptomatic approach is that the body is viewed as a machine, full of moving parts. Each organ can be seen as separate and distinct from other organs. As a result, the medical profession is broken up into specialties.

If you have an emotional problem, you see a psychiatrist; for a foot problem, you see a podiatrist; for a bone problem, you visit an orthopedist; for a nose problem, you go to an ear, nose, and throat specialist; for a heart problem, you visit a cardiologist. And so on.

Viewing the body in such a fragmented way has its consequences.

The various specialties are removed from one another. The heart doctor becomes too busy to concern himself or herself with the study of the liver, while the liver doctor becomes too busy to study the kidney.

A patient with a liver disorder may go to the liver doctor for treatment. The liver doctor prescribes drugs, which make the liver problem go away. But the side effects from the drugs cause heart trouble. So the patient sees a cardiologist, who prescribes heart drugs, and the heart trouble goes away. But those drugs cause kidney disease. The patient then sees a kidney speacialist, who prescribes a drug; the kidney problem goes away, but the drugs cause problems for the spleen. The patient sees a spleen doctor, who prescribes drugs which cure the spleen problem but cause digestive disorders which kill the patient. Each doctor says, "I succeeded," but the patient has died. The reason is that each doctor only saw his or her little part of the body, unable to see that the body is a unity.

The Western medical doctor emphasizes crisis management, as opposed to prevention. He or she works best when there is an acute problem, rather than a chronic illness.

In the end, both Oriental and Occidental physicians are necessary. Both have their strengths and weaknesses. The Oriental healer uses the gentle approach; he or she deals with problems when they are small. The Oriental takes the long view when administering health care and emphasizes the quality of life. The Western medical doctor is highly specific and has the greatest powers in crisis management, dealing with problems when they are large. The Western medical world tends to emphasize the quantity, or longevity, of life.

THE FOUR TYPES OF DIAGNOSIS

The Oriental diagnostician uses four approaches, or ways of assessing another person's health and character. These have Japanese names:

1. *Bo Shin.* Seeing or observing your subject.
2. *Setsu Shin.* Touching your subject, feeling his or her life.
3. *Mon Shin.* Asking questions of your subject to obtain information on his or her condition.
4. *Bun Shin.* Diagnosing through listening and smelling.

Let's look carefully at each of these four approaches.

BO SHIN

There are many synonyms for "seeing." Among them are "observing," "watching," "gazing," "noticing," "perceiving," "visualizing," "star-

ing," and "looking." None of these accurately describes the way of diagnosis using Bo Shin. The closest I can come to it in English is to say that Bo Shin means "to be shown." But as you will soon see, even this is inadequate. We typically think of observing others with our eyes, but I am talking now about observing people with your entire being—seeing another as if your entire body were a set of eyes.

When your patient arrives, greet him or her warmly and be grateful that he or she has come. The person must sense your openness; he or she must recognize your lack of prejudice. You make no judgments or criticisms. Your only desire is to help in your limited way. Together, you and this person will find a way toward better health. You will cooperate with each other. That is the spirit with which you approach this person. You are not superior to him or her in any way. On the contrary, you are grateful that this person has come to you. It is a humbling experience.

Your subject sits before you. You observe the subject as he or she speaks. While your subject is speaking, you must empty yourself. Have no thoughts. Have no preconceptions. Have no resistance to this person. Free yourself from your ego. Become completely empty.

Now let the person's energy, the feeling of his or her personality, wash over you. Let that personality impress itself on you. Let the person's life force affect you. Now you have a sense of his or her vibration.

If you observe too closely, you fail to diagnose using Bo Shin. If you are preoccupied with the shape of your subject's eyes, the color or shape of lips or nose, you have missed the larger picture. The more you focus on details, the more you miss the most meaningful. Leave the details for later. There will be time for them. First, accept your subject's life, his or her vibration. Come to know this person intimately by allowing him or her into your own life force. By doing this, you have taken the first step in making yourself open and receptive to another human being. Nothing remains to block you from understanding this person fully.

Your humility and gratitude are essential to put the person at ease, which will help you in your diagnosis. The more relaxed a person is, the more that person will reveal his or her true nature. If you have ever watched someone sleeping, you know this is true. During sleep, the body naturally assumes a posture that provides the most comfort and healing; the sleeping posture compensates for imbalances in the body that accumulate during the day. But it is a terrible invasion to look at a person sleeping, so you must make your patient unconscious of himself or herself while with you.

In fact, people are unconscious of their bodies most of their waking lives. Consequently, the way they walk, sit, or stand reveals their thinking, their physical discomforts, their aggressiveness or passivity. If they suddenly become self-conscious about the way they walk, sit, or stand, they change to give a different impression of who they are. So you mustn't make your patient feel self-conscious with your observations.

Often the first thing I do is offer my patient tea. At that moment, my whole body is keenly aware. How does he or she accept the cup? How does he or she sit? What are his or her reactions? As we go into the treatment room, I observe my subject closely without his or her being aware of it. In this way, I see the person acting unselfconsciously, and see him or her in a clear light.

In any case, by the time I am ready to give a person Ohashiatsu, I have a pretty good idea about his or her condition.

As my subject opens up and relaxes, I become aware of what I am feeling about him or her. My feelings emerge from within me as I begin to sense this person as a whole.

Sometimes I ask the person to lie on a mat and I cover him or her from head to toe with a sheet. This is so revealing! Now I do not see any details of the person's face or clothes. I do not get distracted by gestures or by a pimple on a cheek. I see only the most obvious contours of the body.

I see where the body bulges, where it is inordinately contracted. I see whether the person lies on the mat straight or curved. Perhaps the back and shoulder region is swollen, or the kidney area is contracted. Perhaps one side of the body is swollen and the other contracted. I see the broader picture. I get a sense of where the problems lie.

Now I let my sense guide me. I place my hands on my patient's back at just the right point, and right away the person says, "Ohashi, thank you so much, that's just where I wanted to be touched. I came here just for that." I massage the body gently, sensing the energy. Now I can move on to my next step.

When you use Bo Shin diagnosis, you are an artist who views another person as a great work of art. You appreciate him or her very deeply, recognizing every nuance, every clue to this person's inner being. To achieve this point of view, you must grow as a person; to truly appreciate the fine points of people, you must elevate your own consciousness.

It is very like learning to appreciate a fine art, like music. When you are a musical novice, many of the finer points of music may be lost on you. But ten years later, you hear things that you never dreamed existed. It is the same with diagnosis. The more you study people, the greater your appreciation of them becomes.

SETSU SHIN

While the literal meaning of Setsu Shin is "touching diagnosis," the deeper meaning is much more abstract. Setsu Shin means contacting the core of the person, touching the inner being of the person. There

is an aspect of Setsu Shin that means "cutting into the core," or "using the hands as if they were knives." This is meant to describe how you pierce the outer layers of another's personality or physical being to go deep within, to touch the inner nature or soul.

Shaking hands is an example of Setsu Shin. Whenever we shake another person's hand, we sense his or her character, we "feel" the inner nature, and we try to communicate our own. A subtle yet profound exchange of information takes place when we shake another person's hand. This is Setsu Shin.

When I give Ohashiatsu I go deeply into the person, probing every fiber and bone, sensing every resistance, every nuance of character. I allow my energy to probe the depths of the person's life. I sense the person's being. It is as if I am bringing my life into this person's life. I am touching his whole life. This is the abstract contact that I make. I am touching the life, the thing we cannot touch.

My fingers and palms become my eyes. I search the person with my hands, my entire being, my own spirit. I try to understand this person on every level—physically, emotionally, psychologically, and spiritually.

You must be open and sensitive to the person. If you are judgmental or critical, the person will close himself or herself off from you. You have failed to make this person accessible to you. You cannot do him or her any good. I say that the person doing the diagnosis is the person being diagnosed. The diagnostician's own shortcomings limit his or her ability to understand the person he or she is trying to help. That is not the subject's fault, but the diagnostician's.

MON SHIN

Asking questions, of course, is the most direct means of assessing the person's health. "Are there any symptoms or personal problems now?" you may ask. You enter into a discussion with your subject.

However, you must listen not only to what is being said, but to what is not being said. You look for the areas this person avoids. You sense the subjects that are sensitive from the way in which your patient discusses them. He or she makes light of a grave issue, perhaps, or glides over a subject that seems significant. Why? You make mental notes.

While the person is speaking, observe whether he or she makes a lot of facial or hand movements. Often, movements are meant to distract others from the point being made. Note the person's body language as you listen carefully to what is being said. Is there a correlation between a specific gesture and an important subject? Do the legs cross, closing off the body, when a sensitive issue is raised? Gently probe with your questions, but if you sense an area a person is avoiding, do not accuse.

Do not force the person into a shell. Your purpose is to gain the person's trust so that you can be of assistance. Know your limits.

BUN SHIN

Defining Bun Shin as "listening diagnosis" is a bit misleading. What I mean by listening is understanding the quality of a person's voice. Once again, you listen with your whole body. Your ear is merely the symbol of the general capacity to hear. The ear is the most specific hearing organ, but the entire body listens and hears. When another person speaks, hear with your body.

When you listen in this way, you will sense the vibration in the person's voice. You allow that vibration to impress itself on your being.

Where does the voice come from? Your first response may be the obvious one, that the voice comes from the larynx, but this is only one of the places from which the voice emanates. If it is a deep voice, it comes from the pit of the stomach or even lower, just below the navel. If a great deal of emotion is carried in the voice, it comes from the heart region. If there is anger in the voice, it comes from the liver. If sympathy is the overriding emotion, the voice comes from the spleen. If there is fear in the voice, it likely indicates a kidney imbalance. If you sense weakness in the voice, it probably comes from the throat. Some voices come from the sinuses or upper head. These are weak, tinny, and thin.

What is the person's dominant feeling as he or she speaks? Does the voice contain laughter, or tears, or anger? Is it a critical voice, an intellectual voice, or a deeply emotional voice?

The voice reveals so much about the person's current mental, emotional, and physical health. A person can choose words that cover deeper feelings. A patient may try to hide his or her real feelings, but the voice gives much away. Listen carefully to it. Allow it to tell you how well or ill the person really feels.

Bun Shin also includes smell diagnosis. For you to smell another person's body clearly, your own health and condition must be very clean. You cannot smell something being discharged by another person when you are discharging that same thing from your body. I am Japanese; therefore, I cannot smell Japanese people very well, but I am keenly aware of the smell of Americans and Europeans.

If you eat lots of unhealthy foods, fat, and sugar, you cannot smell these foods being discharged by another person's body. But if your condition is clean, you can smell very well what other people are eliminating.

In general, people who eat a great deal of animal food have a stronger smell because their bodies are filled with ammonia. Protein foods break down in the body into ammonia, which is highly toxic and has a foul smell. These people often cover their bodies with heavy deodorants, perfumes, and colognes. If a person gives off a powerful cologne smell, it often indicates that the person's own capacity to smell is weak, and that his or her personal odor is strong, prompting him or her to splash cologne on too heavily.

Hormonal imbalances can be smelled as a slightly burnt odor, foul from the fat and ammonia that are the cause of the hormonal imbalance.

Fat becomes rancid in the body and emits an odor of rancidity, as if something has gone bad.

To develop your capacity for smell diagnosis, you should eat a diet made up primarily of whole grains, vegetables, and small amounts of fish. Grains, vegetables, beans, and other plant foods give off water and carbon dioxide when they are burned as fuel, constituents that are easily eliminated from the body without much effort—or smell.

Remember, when you diagnose someone, you enter that person's private world. You ask the person to allow you further into that world so that you can be of assistance. This requires a highly developed sense of propriety and manners. You must have the noblest intentions. Oriental diagnosis is a delicate art that must be carried out with respect for other human beings and their right to privacy.

The most appropriate attitude you can have when diagnosing another person is love. The greater your love for this person, the more you will see in him or her, and the more the person will allow you to know.

2

How Can
the Body Be Read?

THE FIRST QUESTION YOU WILL BE ASKING YOURSELF AS you examine this book is, How can a specific line on someone's face, or the shape of his or her nose, indicate anything about the person's health or character?

In the modern world, there are no answers to such questions, but in the Orient, as well as in many traditional Western cultures, a fundamental philosophy exists whose application reveals the meaning behind each of our physical features. I am talking about the philosophy of yin and yang.

Let us, then, begin our understanding of Oriental diagnosis by learning about yin and yang.

YIN AND YANG: THE FORCES OF CHANGE

Yin and yang can be seen as the powers that make physical reality possible. They are the tools of God, so to speak. Without these two opposites—in the forms of time and space, light and dark, male and female, and dimension (for example, near and far, up and down, left and right)—nothing in the physical world would be possible. People in all ancient cultures realized this. In fact, the Bible begins:

> In the beginning God created the heavens and the earth. . . . Then God said, "Let there be light": and there was light. And God saw that the light was good; and God separated the light from the darkness.

And He called the light day, and the darkness He called night. And
there was evening and there was morning, one day.

Everything God made was composed of opposites—heaven and
earth, light and dark, morning and evening, land and ocean, male and
female.

In the old days, the sages studied these opposites to understand their
natures. They found that in the heavens were the sun, the moon, the
stars, and the planets, all showering energy down on the earth in the
form of sunlight, cosmic rays, and gravitational forces. Other forces
emanated from the heavens as well: the wind, weather, seasons, and
climates. These forces came from above and followed a downward path
toward the earth; they were called yang.

In general, the yang force causes things to contract, or grow closer
to the earth. Gravity, for example, is yang.

The sages found that the earth, on the other hand, had an entirely
different nature. It spun on its axis, causing energy to fly outward and
upward toward the heavens. The sages called this force yin. It had an
expansive influence.

Things that grow upward—such as trees and many plants—are yin.

Contraction, or the yang force, occurs in the centripetal spiral—that
is, a spiral that tightens or contracts toward the center. Expansion, the
yin force, occurs in a centrifugal spiral, or one that opens and expands
away from the center.

Yin and yang have other characteristics. Yin things are more passive,
lighter, porous, and moist, while yang things are more active, heavier,
dense, and dry. When you blow up a balloon, you are making it more
yin. Nighttime is less active and less charged with energy than daytime;
it is the more yin part of the day. The female sex is the more yin.
Heaven, as the creator of all things, is the more active element, or more
yang, while the earth, the recipient of heaven, the more passive element,
is more yin.

Things that expand from the earth are becoming more yin, while
things that are pressed downward on the earth are becoming more
yang. Tall people are generally more yin than short people; the more
thin, frail, or small-boned a person is, the more yin he or she is said
to be.

Yin people like to work with their heads, rather than their hands.
They enjoy office work more than, say, ditch digging or house building.
(When I discuss the shape of the face and head from the yin and yang
perspective, you will see more clearly the differences between yin and
yang constitutions.) Those with yin constitutions prefer the indoors.
Yin people are more introverted.

People with yang constitutions are generally shorter and bigger-
boned. They tend to be more active and physically oriented. They like

to work with their hands. They enjoy the outdoors; they love to be with people. They are more extroverted.

Everything possesses both yin and yang within itself. For example, the yin part of a tree is the branches and leaves—the part that stretches upward and outward—while the most yang part is the root system. The trunk is also yang, but the bottom of the trunk is more yang than the top.

Each of us possesses degrees of both yin and yang. For many, both yin and yang exist in extremes. Basketball players are examples of extremes of yin and yang. They are tall, but big-boned, extremely strong, and active.

Everything in the human body functions by virtue of yin and yang. The heart, for example, pumps blood through its ability to contract (yang) and expand (yin); the lungs breathe air through their ability to contract and expand; the muscles of the body function through expansion and contraction. Yin and yang are everywhere in the human body, as well as in every activity we perform during the day and night.

The important point here is that we need to live according to our natures. If a man or woman is more yin in nature, he or she will be most unhappy working in construction or any other profession that is extremely yang. The opposite is also true; yang people suffer badly if you force them to sit at a desk all day.

Yin and yang can also be applied to specific areas of the body. For example, the head is the more yin part of the body, the feet the more yang. Thinking takes place in the head; thoughts, which are intangible, ephemeral, and changing, are extremely yin forms of energy. On the other hand, the feet rest on the earth, which is solid, stable, material, and firm—all very yang characteristics.

The outer part of the body is more yin than the interior, the upper part more yin than the lower.

The environment, our activities or life-style, and the food we eat affect our bodies, causing us to expand or contract. Exercise, for example, has a yang, or contractive effect; it makes muscles tight and strong, as opposed to loose, expanded, and flabby. Certain foods, such as salt, meat, and hard cheese, have a yang effect, while other food and drink, such as fruit, fruit juice, sugar, and alcohol, have a more yin, or expansive, effect on our thinking and on our bodies. Sugar and alcohol, for example, cause our thinking to become less focused and intense and our bodies to become less coordinated and more out of control. The overconsumption of meat or other proteinaceous foods causes us to think and act more aggressively and to try to exert more control over our environment. Whole grains are thought to be at the center of the yin-yang spectrum; fish is slightly yang, beans and vegetables slightly yin.

Yin influences tend to affect the top part of the body, from the solar plexus up, while yang influences tend to affect the lower part of the body, from the solar plexus down. As every cardiologist knows, salt (a very yang food) tends to affect kidneys, while alcohol (a very yin substance) has a direct and immediate effect on the brain and nervous system.

One of the laws of Oriental diagnosis that I will repeat thoughout this book is that the macro can be seen in the micro. Yin and yang make this possible. The face, for example, has a yin part and a yang part. If you draw a line across the middle of the face, from the bottom of one ear to the bottom of the other, the part above that line is the yin part of the face, and the part below is the yang part. The yin part of the face—the cheekbones, nose, eyes, forehead, and scalp—represents the yin part of the body—the lungs, heart, liver, and nervous system. The area including the mouth represents the more yang or lower part of the body, meaning the intestines, and sex organs. It is the same throughout the body.

As we progress through the book, I will talk a lot about the ways in which our life-styles, activities, and diets affect our lives according to the ways in which they change the balance of yin and yang within us.

For now, it is important to know that the body is a totality, an integrated system. That system is continually influenced by yin and yang, with first one dominating, then the other. By understanding our own peculiar imbalances, we can come to understand ourselves at a much deeper level, and learn to take action that restores harmony and balance to our lives. In this way, we can help other people heal themselves, or direct them toward a happier life.

True insight into the nature of other people and of ourselves depends on our ability to understand yin and yang and how they manifest in each person we deal with.

Throughout this book, I will apply yin and yang to specific facial and body features, as well as to the overall constitution. In the process, you will see the meaning behind each of our physical characteristics.

Let's begin by examining the ways in which yin and yang can be used to discern character, talents, and health from the features of the face.

THE FACE

When it comes to reading another person's feelings, or sensing his or her character, the face is the most revealing part of the human body. Even those who know nothing of Oriental diagnosis study others' faces when trying to discern their thoughts on important matters. The face is the most sensitive and responsive part of the body. No other external part of the body reveals so obviously the subtle changes within.

Why is this so? One reason is that the face is a complex web of muscles. In the face and cranium alone, there are ten muscle systems, totaling nearly forty individual muscles in all. These muscles give the face great flexibility and highly articulate expression.

Besides its muscle systems, the face has a dramatic mix of features—the eyes, nose, mouth, eyebrows, and jaw—each capable of a wide range of movement and nuance. As every gambler knows, these features alone provide a great deal of information about how a person is feeling. In a single glance, the face can speak volumes without its owner's uttering a single word.

The head (including the face and ears) is the sensory center of the body. The eyes, nose, mouth, and ears provide four of the five tactile senses.

These organs also provide the entrances to larger systems. The mouth is the entrance to the digestive tract; the nose, to respiration; the eyes, to the optic nerve, brain, and nervous system; the ears, to hearing. Obviously, a clear relationship exists between each entranceway and the system itself: when the respiratory system and sinuses fill with mucus, the nose tends to run. When the digestion is troubled, we often have a bad taste in the mouth. Nervousness or tension is often revealed in the eyes. These are just a few of the more obvious signs people use to detect another person's inner condition.

But apart from these ordinary bits of information is the larger truth about the face, which is that unless you are a pathological liar, you find it difficult to prevent your face from revealing your feelings. Your happiness shows; your unhappiness shows. So too do your boredom and embarrassment, your concentration and consternation, your sickness and health. Your face is honest. It reveals the truth of the inner you. This is true even when we would like it to be otherwise, and it is why people naturally study another person's face to discern his or her character, thoughts, and inner nature.

In the Orient, we have a bit of folk wisdom that says that by the age of forty you are responsible for your own face. This means that while you are a child, an adolescent, and even a young adult, your face is still the result of your family heritage and environment, but by the time you are forty you have lived long enough on your own to have created yourself; you are an adult, fully responsible for your own condition, and your own face.

As you grow older, your character gradually emerges; the principles to which you truly subscribe become etched on your face. These principles are not necessarily the ones you would admit to. Gradually, the social, political, and economical conditions of your life are sculpted on your face. We can perceive all sorts of characteristics in people's faces: intelligence and dullness, charisma and self-hatred, honesty and dishonesty. We perceive these things even when we know nothing of the person we are looking at.

By the time you are forty, your character shows. But this does not mean that your face is finished—you and it have a long way to go. But now you are fully responsible for what you are and will become.

The uniqueness of each face is astounding. There is no way to adequately express this fact. The creativity of the universe is awesome. When I walk down the street in Tokyo, I am amazed at the uniqueness and complexity in Japanese faces. Yet these facial characteristics have many similarities. After all, virtually all Japanese have black hair (except, of course, for those whose hair is gray), yellow skin, and dark eyes. The men are of similar height, weight, and build. Many similarities exist among the women as well. And yet no two faces are alike. Each bears its own unique character.

If you walk down the street in New York, you are confronted with a rainbow of skin colors, nationalities, heights, weights, and shapes. The mind boggles. What an infinite marvel! This astounding variety has been created with the same basic elements—two eyes, one nose, one mouth, and an irregular ball of a head.

You may wonder: Given this enormous diversity, how is it possible to say anything about the human face, except that each one is unique?

Here is another remarkable paradox: within diversity we find remarkable consistency. The human body is shaped by universal law. We know that DNA ensures the integrity of the basic human form. But what ensures the integrity of the basic shape of DNA? The answer is the invisible law that shapes the universe. This law itself is a product of the Great Spirit, which is infinitely creative, yet remarkably consistent. It forms the real foundation of life. Biological life is but a symptom of the underlying law of the universe. If you study the symptoms, or the outward manifestations, of life, what will be revealed to you is the unseen nature of things beneath the surface.

In the Orient, this underlying law or spirit is often called Tao. In the West, of course, it is called God. Tao or God cannot be described. It is beyond comprehension. What can be described is the law by which it operates. In the Orient, we know this law as yin and yang.

As I mentioned earlier, yin and yang are diametrical opposites. They are complementary yet opposing forces that combine to form all phenomena.

The first thing you must realize is that most of us are combinations of yin and yang. We have degrees of passivity, openness, and intellectual development on the yin side of the spectrum, while at the same time we also have yang characteristics, such as aggression, self-motivation, and focus. Generally, however, our constitutions are imbalanced in favor of the yin or yang side.

In developing self-understanding and knowledge, we must come to know which of our characteristics are yin and yang and act accordingly. Ideally, we strive for balance between the two to create the greatest harmony and peace within.

We can learn a lot about the balance of yin and yang by observing the shape and characteristics of the head. We can learn even more by studying the individual features of the face.

It is important to keep in mind the distinction between constitutional traits, or characteristics shaped by our genes, and conditional traits, or characteristics that change day to day, week to week, or month to month. Constitutional characteristics are given to us at birth; blood type, sex, and inborn health—these tend to be inherited. Genetic or constitutional traits reveal our underlying nature. There are no bad natures, no bad constitutional traits. In Oriental diagnosis, everything has the potential for good, and, as I have said, it all depends on how we view the characteristic and use the ability it indicates. Genetic traits cannot be changed. They can only be brought to fruition or repressed. Constitutional characteristics indicate much about the fundamentally spiritual beings we are.

However, we have many conditional, or temporary, traits that indicate much about our current physical, mental, and spiritual health. These characteristics change all the time. Such things as a temporary profusion of red blood vessels in the eyes; a rash or blemish on the face; a swelling in a particular part of the body, such as under the eyes—these reveal the current state of our health. We can change these characteristics by changing life-style patterns, such as exercise, ways of eating, and ways of thinking.

Our health tends to be stronger and more vital when our lives are appropriate for our constitutional characteristics. If your nature is to be a musician but you work as a construction engineer, you will suffer health disorders, especially if the situation causes you severe conflict. You will see what I mean more clearly as I move on to the next topic, the constitutional traits revealed in the size and shape of the head.

THE YIN FACE AND CHARACTER

The shape of the yin face generally resembles an upside-down teardrop, large at the forehead area and narrow at the chin. The forehead is high and broad. The yin person has large eyes and rounded eyebrows that usually arch higher above the nose and slope downward toward the outside edge of the face. The eyebrows are often wide apart. The yin face is usually narrow. So, too, are the bridge of the nose and the nostrils. The yin face has pale skin; the cheekbones do not look very high or developed.

Writers Tom Wolfe and Joyce Carol Oates, Austrian president Kurt Waldheim, and cartoon character Olive Oyl all have variations of the yin face.

Yin face.

The mouth in a yin face is moderately wide and the lips rather pale, owing to a lack of circulation. In general, yin people have poorer blood circulation, which makes their bodies colder; as a result, they dislike cold weather and are prone to remain indoors. They abhor hard physical labor.

The yin body is lean and sometimes frail. Rarely is a yin person overweight.

Yin people tend to have small appetites, but their approach to food usually goes to one of two extremes: either they become passionate connoisseurs of food and wine or they are indifferent, viewing food in strictly utilitarian terms. The yin type rarely finds himself or herself in the middle. Whichever extreme they follow, yin people as a rule prefer sweet and softer foods. In general, they have weak digestion and often suffer from diarrhea.

The yin person has a refined disposition and a softer voice and is usually gentle. Yin types are extremely sensitive, especially to their own emotions. Though they are often highly emotional people, they have some difficulty expressing feelings. They tend to be caught up in their own pasts, especially in painful events. Yin people are given to melancholy and depression; they see the world as a place of struggle and pain, and sometimes doubt that any of it has much meaning. They can be timid and occasionally withdrawn. They tend to be introverts. They must avoid the victim mentality, which can be a stumbling block in the road to success.

Yin types are highly intellectual, approaching life through the mind; they are often smart and articulate. Because they are so sensitive, life at times seems to them unduly harsh and overwhelming, causing many to escape to their intellects to deal with the suffering with which life presents them. At such times, the yin type may seem so intellectual as to be removed from much of human experience.

People with yin constitutions usually possess highly sensitive intuition. If they can go beyond their own emotional centers, they can become veritable radar detectors in discerning other people's moods, attitudes, or thoughts.

Yin people tend to be spiritually oriented. They are drawn to religious, philosophical, and mystical areas of study. Their intuition and sensitivity lead them to investigate dreams, visions, and deeper psychological and spiritual themes. If they can remain grounded in reality, yin people make wonderful psychological counselors.

Their acute sensitivity and intuitiveness are very often revealed as highly refined artistic talent. Yin people are often writers, painters, or musicians. They possess the ability to express the more subtle aspects of human experience.

People with yin constitutions enjoy staying out late at night. They are coffee and wine drinkers and especially enjoy late-night discussions.

Their hours generally violate the hours of nature; they go to bed late and often are still awake in the small hours of the morning. Consequently, they have trouble getting out of bed in the morning. They are also lighter sleepers and usually need time to fall asleep.

Sometimes you see someone with a narrow yin face and a strong, athletic body. This combination of yin head and yang body type signifies the presence of two extremes within the same person, which can present the person with some difficult contradictions. Such people find themselves attracted to more yin ways, such as a passionate interest in food, late hours, and a passive life-style, but also feel drawn to more yang ways, such as participation in athletics, much physical contact, and an active life-style. These people must work hard to achieve balance. If they do not recognize this need, and do not take the appropriate actions, they will suffer from health problems.

Those with yin constitutions must carefully guard their health. Yin people tend to have fragile constitutions to begin with, and their love of rich foods, sweets, wine, and stimulants can lead to a variety of digestive disorders, and diseases of the spleen, lymphatic system, and kidney.

Yin people must also avoid a kind of yin arrogance—a feeling of aloof superiority. Yin people can fall victim to the attitude that the rest of the world is beneath them, either intellectually or culturally. They can easily be perceived as snobs.

To maintain health and equlibrium, the yin person needs exercise and a balanced diet (see chapter 9, "A Program for Better Health"). Regular walking, running, and sports (such as tennis, basketball, racquetball, and swimming) are excellent. Moreover, the yin person should get out in nature and continually experience the elements—the cold, rain, sun, and earth. He or she must cultivate tolerance and endurance. The yin person's body must be felt and strengthened to balance the natural inclination to reside solely in the mind.

THE YANG FACE AND CHARACTER

The yang face is round to square, with a wide jaw that gives the appearance of strength. The face is more balanced than the yin face between the forehead and jaw. In the extremely yang face the jaw may appear wider than the top of the head.

The yang-faced person has a wide mouth; when the yang type is healthy, the lips look full and red. The nose is wide, with flared nostrils. The yang person's eyes tend to be medium-sized to small, under thick eyebrows which usually lie close together over the bridge of the nose. The yang forehead is average to small. The yang face tends to be red; occasionally veins appear on the surface of the skin around the eyes or nose.

Yang faces include former U.S. president Ronald Reagan (a square-

Yang face.

faced yang), Soviet president Mikhail Gorbachev (a round-faced yang), German chancellor Helmut Kohl (also round-faced), CBS football analyst John Madden (with a big square head and a jaw that seems wider than his forehead), operatic tenor Luciano Pavarotti (with a huge round head and a wide jaw), and operatic soprano Beverly Sills (also round-headed).

Yang people have strong appetites and excellent digestion, which they often abuse. They eat great quantities of food, are effusive in their praise of it and of the cook, and then light up a cigar when the meal is concluded. They are adventurous in their eating, experimenting widely for no other reason than to have a new experience. They especially enjoy spicy, rich cuisine. Yang people love food, but they are not likely to become connoisseurs. They don't have to; they love everything they eat.

The yang person also has a large appetite for beer and hard liquor.

The yang person often has a strong voice; many yang men, in fact, have voices that boom.

Yang people have strong, often muscular bodies, but they tend to become overweight. Ironically, yang people's large appetites do not usually attract them to drugs; they love to taste their excesses, and drugs tend to dull taste.

Yang people are demonstrative in love. They have strong emotions and a strong sex drive. They have no trouble showing their feelings, either in love or anger, and when riled sufficiently can become violent.

The yang person falls asleep easily, sleeps deeply, and adheres to the cycles of nature. Yang people get sleepy before midnight and naturally awaken with the rise of the sun. They get to work early and maintain great vitality through the course of the day.

A yang person can easily become a workaholic, focusing exclusively on the goal ahead and blocking out distractions. At times, those distractions can include family, friends, and the yang person's own health, making him or her susceptible to breakdowns.

The yang type enjoys physical labor, sports, and the great outdoors. Yang people like the challenge of the outdoors and love nature. They prefer cooler temperatures to hot.

Yang people may not always be sensitive. To many—especially very yin people—they appear downright insensitive. Yang people tend to get right to the point, avoiding diplomacy except when it suits them. They can be gruff and overbearing, even brutish. Yang people must avoid becoming bullies. Their strength gives them the impression that they can force events and people into line. This makes them susceptible to becoming overly manipulative, and may draw them into power politics, usually resulting in their own destruction at some point down the line.

I advise yang people that they must avoid becoming arrogant, overly aggressive, and angry.

Thanks to their love of fatty foods, alcohol, and tobacco, yang people are most susceptible to heart disease, high blood pressure, and diseases of the colon, especially colon cancer. Here is an example of how a strength can become a weakness. Yang types have naturally strong digestion, but because of this strength they tend to abuse themselves with food and drink, causing digestive disorders. If they lived moderately—a condition forced on those who are naturally less strong—they would not be tempted to eat and drink so abusively.

Yang people should eat only small amounts of red meat, spices, and baked goods, and should limit their indulgence in hard alcohol. They need to avoid fatty foods and those rich in cholesterol, eating more whole grains and leafy greens, which provide fiber that aids digestion.

The yang type needs restful pastimes, soft music, and lots of plants to generate oxygen in the home. Gardening, prayer, and meditation can provide a wonderful balance for the yang person's natural aggressiveness.

Yang people need to appreciate the yin things in life—the gentleness and love of family, the restfulness of nature, and the peace of prayer. Yang people must recognize their limitations—not an easy thing to do for such types—lest they burn out.

THE THREE ZONES OF THE FACE: FOREHEAD, MID-REGION, AND JAW

As everyone knows, the heads of prehistoric humans were very different from those of modern people. Archaeologists have discovered skulls and bone fragments two to three million years old from a human ancestor called *Australopithecus africanus,* which had characteristics similar to those of apes: no forehead at all (reflecting the fact that *A. africanus* had a very small brain, and did very little thinking with what he had), a wide nose, and a large, wide jaw that jutted forward from the rest of the face, with large teeth. In the head of *A. africanus,* the area below the nose commands the most attention.

Two million years ago, an early human ancestor called *Homo habilis* emerged, with a somewhat larger brain and the early signs of a forehead. One and a half million years ago, *Homo habilis* was followed by *Homo erectus,* who had further brain and skull development, including a more pronounced forehead. Finally, some five hundred thousand years ago, we, *Homo sapiens,* came on the scene. We, of course, have considerable brain development (evidence to the contrary notwithstanding) and a very straight forehead. In comparison with that of our earliest ancestors,

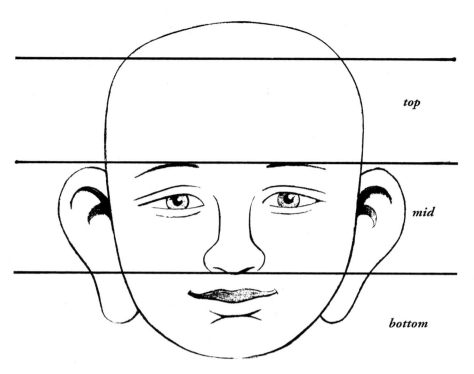

The three sections of the face: top section, between the hairline and the eyebrows; middle section, between the eyebrows and the bottom of the nose; bottom section, below the nose.

the mid-region of our face is more refined and more pronounced. Our jaws are getting smaller; we are no longer all eyes and jaws, as our prehistoric forebears were.

The early forerunners of human beings were hunter-gatherers whose primary mission in life was survival. It wasn't astrophysics, or literature, or medicine that dominated our ancestors' lives: it was eating and struggling against the hostile environment. Since eating commanded so much of their energy and attention, it's not surprising that their faces were dominated by the mouth and jaw.

Survival is still an important mission in the modern world, but we have other needs as well—complex emotional, psychological, and spiritual needs of which our earliest ancestors had no inkling.

My point here is to show that there has always been a clear relationship between human physiognomy or facial features, and human characteristics. As the brain developed, and with it the intellect, so too did the size of the head and forehead. Other characteristics changed as well, as emotionally and psychologically, humans became more complex. As we will see, this too is reflected in the face.

Remember that one of the cardinal laws of Oriental diagnosis is that the macro can be seen in the micro. When we apply this law to the face, we see that the state of the entire body is revealed there.

In my classes, I often draw a face on the blackboard and then superimpose on it a small stick-figure drawing, creating a small man or
woman drawn within the circle of the larger face. The head of the stick
figure is drawn over the forehead, the spine over the bridge of the nose,
the waist above the mouth, and the legs running to the chin.

This drawing illustrates the way in which the organs of the body are
revealed on the face. The stick figure's head, drawn over the forehead,
shows that our thinking and intellectual development can be seen on
our foreheads. The curvature of the spine can be read along the bridge
of the nose, the intestines at the mouth, and the genital region in the
area above and just below the mouth.

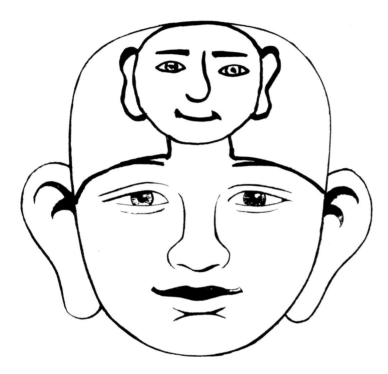

The micro represents the macro. If you project the entire body onto the face, the nose
represents the spine.

I will discuss each area of the face, and its corresponding organs and
systems, in due course, but for now let's look at the three regions of
the face—the forehead, mid-region, and jaw—and the information each
provides.

1. The forehead shows the intellectual nature.
2. The mid-region, between the eyes and mouth, shows the emotional
    nature.
3. The chin and jaw, including the area below the nose and around
    the mouth, show the strength of the will.

One of the first things we look for when we examine a person's face is the relative size of these three areas. Does one dominate the face—the forehead, for example—or are they relatively equal in size?

THE BALANCED FACE

If the three areas of the face are equally large or small, the individual possesses a balanced nature. He or she is not dominated by the mind, heart, or will, but, instead, attempts to make rational decisions based on a harmony among these three aspects of being.

Balanced features are not as common as you might think; usually one region of the face dominates. Occasionally you see someone with a balanced face and a large, round head. Such people tend to be visionaries with tremendous power. They possess a rare blend of intellectual development, understanding of the emotional needs of people, and strong will. They tend to have a philosophical turn of mind, yet they possess the will and the courage to bring their plans to fruition. They are practical idealists, bound for high accomplishment. They are farsighted and have good social judgment and endurance.

Some examples of balanced faces include Winston Churchill, Mikhail Gorbachev, Governor of New York Mario Cuomo, and former Secretary of State Henry Kissinger.

Such people have an Achilles heel: arrogance. When they begin to realize their potential, they can see themselves as superior to others, which heralds their defeat. The person with a round head and balanced face must remain a part of the human race to draw strength from it and guide others. To hold on to popular support, he or she must identify strongly with the needs of others.

THE HIGH FOREHEAD

Sometimes you see someone with a very high forehead, a smaller midregion, and an even smaller chin. This is the typical yin face. The yin type is dominated by the intellect; the emotions are strong, but not nearly as strong as the mind. The willpower is the weakest aspect of the character. This type of person is highly intellectual, even brilliant. Yin people have conceptual minds; they can be great planners or abstract thinkers, and can serve as advisers to powerful leaders. The yin-faced person possesses visionary and spiritual ideals.

These people must guard against becoming aloof, overly intellectual, critical, or cynical, and must avoid intrigues or struggles for power. In the end, the yin-faced person will lose such battles, especially if he or she attempts to supplant a strong leader. The yin person usually cannot endure the demands of leadership; the will is weak, and the emotions override it. The yin person cannot realize the grand visions his or her

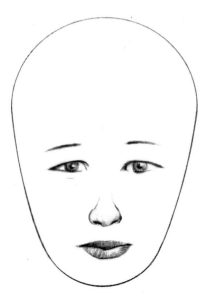

The high forehead: the top section dominates the face.

mind conjures up; for that, the yin person needs the help of more yang people.

THE WELL-DEVELOPED MID-REGION

A person whose face is dominated by the mid-region is very emotional, solicitous, even sentimental. Such people make wonderful nurses, healers, or therapists. They sympathize with the pain of others. They understand the suffering of life and seek to heal it. They have a highly developed maternal nature.

People with large mid-regions are often artistic as well. They have a fine sense of beauty, especially in the more physical arts, such as sculpture, dance, and painting.

These people's chief weakness is that they can be thrown about by their feelings. They can be mercurial, flying off the handle one moment and placid the next, exploding with joy and happiness or plunging into depression. These emotional people need to develop a sense of reason, a businesslike approach to work, and a willingness to endure, especially when faced with conflicts in relationships.

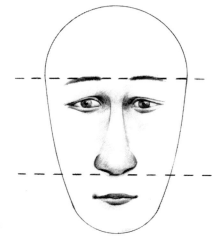

The big center: the middle section dominates the face.

THE BIG JAW

A person with a pronounced jaw has a powerful will and a strong sense of purpose. This is a typical yang face. He or she can endure conflict and remain focused on his or her goal. Such people are practical, goal-oriented, often workaholics; they wish to dominate their little corner of the earth in some fashion. Jaw-dominated people have great courage and tenacity; they will fight until the battle is won.

People with strong jaws can be materialistic and status-conscious. They want it known that they possess the best of everything. Such people may be extremely willful and stubborn. They often ignore the ideas or feelings of others to follow their own course. In a conflict, such people will try to bulldoze their way through things, or will ignore their enemies, pretending that they simply do not exist.

The person whose jaw dominates his or her face tends to see things in black and white, and to see others as either for them or against them. For these people there is no middle road. Such people are often very attached to their personal goals, often to the exclusion of other needs. The jaw-dominated person must develop compassion and human understanding. Out of these ideas will come a greater appreciation for the deeper meanings of life.

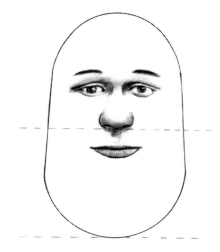

The big jaw: the lower section dominates the face.

INDIVIDUAL FEATURES OF THE FACE

Most of us are not so exclusively yin or yang as those with the facial types I've just discussed. We possess degrees of both yin and yang, which show themselves in various features of our faces and bodies. In this section, I'll describe specific yin and yang characteristics they suggest. Let's begin by looking at the details of the forehead.

THE FOREHEAD AND ITS LINES

Everyone has lines on his or her forehead. Most of us take these lines for granted and see them as meaningless. But for the Oriental diagnostician, these lines have great significance.

Lines on the forehead are a product of our nervous system. They relate to the activities of the forebrain, which is directly behind the forehead. Orderly brain development and activity affect the shape of the whole head, especially the forehead, and the lines that appear there, as do disorderly brain development and brain activity, in the form of electrical brain waves, which reveal disorderly and chaotic lines.

As with other characteristics of the body, yin and yang can be used to reveal much about specific lines. For example, the uppermost line on the forehead correlates with the most yin aspects of personality, while the lowest correlates with the most yang. The top line, therefore, represents our spiritual nature, while the bottom represents our relationship with the earth. But let's look at the specific lines on the forehead and examine their particular meanings in Oriental diagnosis.

Three archetypal lines run across the forehead. Ideally, they are long, straight, and unbroken. Some people have only one or two lines on the forehead, while others have more than three. These variations, too, are revealing, but let's begin with the basics.

The three archetypal lines represent the three levels of human existence. The top line represents heaven, or the person's spiritual nature; the condition of this line reveals his or her attitudes toward the higher ideal of human life. The middle line represents the human personality, the strength or weakness of the ego. The bottom line represents the earth and the person's relationship with practical, earthly matters, including work and finances. This line often shows the person's capacity to realize his or her ideas.

If all three lines are distinct, unbroken, and strong, the person possesses a balanced view of himself or herself in relationship to spiritual, ego, and earthly roles. Such a person experiences little conflict between spiritual and earthly needs. He or she also has a strong sense of self and the potential to attain an integrated personality. The presence of three deep, clear lines indicates good health and basically sound judg-

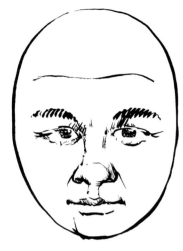

One unbroken line: steady health, consistent life energy.

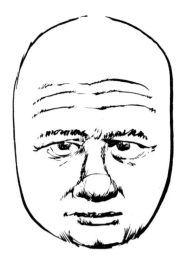

Many unbroken lines: inconsistent health, many interests.

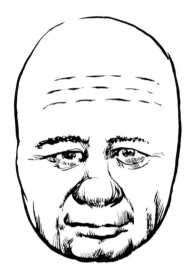

Broken lines: unreliable personality, changing health condition.

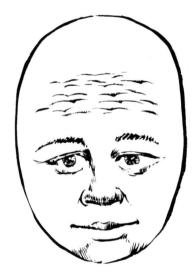

"Flying bird" broken lines: extreme personality, continually changing or unstable health.

ment. As long as such a person takes care of his or her health and exercises good judgment, he or she will likely fare well in life.

Breaks in any of the three lines indicate a problem or conflict in the aspect of life which that line represents. Broken lines suggest that the person will have to work a little harder—sometimes a lot harder—to gain mastery over that part of life. A broken line often shows where a person's focus in life is. He or she feels compelled to accomplish something in this area. This part of life requires greater effort and more attention than other parts.

A broken earth line means that the person must take good care of earthly and material matters, working at maintaining steady income, balancing the checkbook, and maintaining an orderly work schedule. Such a person will have to consciously develop good habits to sustain any sort of security in what is otherwise, an unpredictable world. People with broken earth lines joined with strong heaven and personality lines are often working to realize some idealistic goal or vision.

Broken lines indicate intermittent concerns about health. Sometimes the person will enjoy strong health and vitality; at other times, he or she will suffer some illness. Eventually, he or she will recover and once again experience good health. In other words, health is a roller-coaster ride for those with broken forehead lines.

Occasionally you see a person whose forehead has very wavy lines, indicating regular changes in health and imbalanced thinking. Such a person has a hard time making up his or her mind and sticking to a particular direction in life. These people change jobs, spouses, and partners often. They never seem sure. They are always wondering if the grass isn't greener over the next hill.

A missing line reveals a lack of interest, even a blind spot, in the part of life represented by the absent line. This blind spot can lead the person to the erroneous belief that certain questions in life are unimportant or irrelevant to his or her existence.

A missing line can also have the opposite meaning. It can signify a much deeper concern for the aspect of life represented by the line. As if aware of the blind spot, the person may find this aspect mysterious and exciting and may therefore put greater effort into exploring it. Such a person can become deeply intrigued, even obsessed, with such matters.

Let's assume that a person has strong, unbroken top and middle lines, representing spirituality and personality, but is missing the bottom line, having to do with earthly matters. This person has a solid sense of self; he or she is likely to be emotionally balanced and highly idealistic. This person may even attain a leading position in some idealistic cause. However, he or she is likely to have an imbalanced view of earthly concerns, especially business and money. He or she may view the world as tainted, seeing business and financial affairs as ultimately unspiritual or unidealistic. Such a person will have trouble, therefore, manifesting his or her higher ideals in the material world. He or she may experience frustration, especially later in life. This person must learn that the practical, economic lessons of life are spiritual lessons, too, and that to change the world for the better, we must join the higher and the lower, marrying the higher human ideals with the bottom line.

If a person has no spiritual line, but deep personality and earthly lines, he or she has a strong sense of self, potential for leadership, and materialistic goals that are not necessarily balanced by spiritual ideals.

Such a person may view spiritually oriented people as impractical, or even as kooks. People with strong personality and earth lines tend to be corporate types or entrepreneurs. They avoid matters of the spirit, focusing instead on career concerns, personal ambition, and the goals of their employers.

Sometimes you see a person with only one clear line. If it is the personality line, the person has a strong sense of self; he or she may present a powerful presence and be much admired. This person may be oriented toward spiritual matters or earthly matters.

Egotism is a great danger to such people, leading them to believe that they are above spiritual and earthly matters. Since they have no ideals to balance them, they can fill their lives with intrigues. They may also be possessed by ambition, but not necessarily because they love material objects or seek career advancement. On the contrary, they may be indifferent to possessions, except as status symbols, regarding possessions and achievements as proof of their superiority.

People with one strong personality line, however, tend to be leaders and have charisma, which, when used properly, can motivate others toward a single goal.

Those with only a heaven line are highly idealistic but impractical. They must work at developing their own personalities, their sense of self, and their understanding of the earth.

Those with only an earth line see life largely in terms of their material security. They regard matters of the spirit as highly abstract and irrelevant to daily life.

Sometimes you see a person with two distinct horizontal lines, one just above each eyebrow. These are known as intuition lines. The person with such lines has a marked degree of intuition, sound judgment when it comes to assessing the character of others, and high spiritual ideals. These lines are the sign of a person who has worked hard on himself or herself and made significant progress.

Between the eyebrows, just above the nose, you will see a variety of vertical lines. These lines reveal the condition of the liver.

Before I explain these lines, I must discuss another important point in Oriental healing so that you can better understand the liver and other organs. Many centuries ago, Oriental healers developed an understanding of the body as an integrated whole. Psychological stability—especially emotional stability—depended on the healthy functioning of the entire body, including every individual organ. Each organ played a specific role in overall health and in the stability of a specific emotion. The liver, for example, controlled anger. A person who injured his or her liver through unhealthy eating and drinking, for example, suffered from acute anger and hostility. Often such people would explode with unexplainable anger; this revealed the presence of an unhealthy liver. Rather than talk endlessly about the person's psychological state, the healer would treat the liver and the anger would diminish.

One of the ways a healer would diagnose a liver problem was to look at the area just above the nose, between the eyebrows.

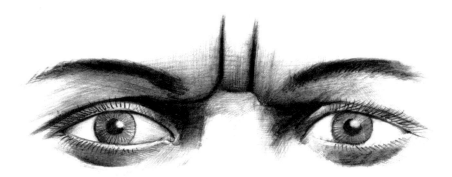

Deep vertical lines between the eyes: tension, anger, nervousness, liver problems.

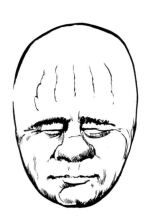

Many vertical lines on the forehead: intelligent, critical, very cautious, thinks a lot.

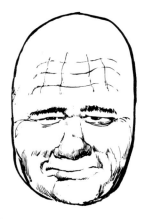

Vertical and horizontal lines: extremely intelligent, or extremely sensitive and nervous, or both.

Most people have two parallel vertical lines here. These lines should be light and shallow, indicating that the liver is functioning well. If the lines are deep, the liver is somewhat troubled and congested. The person will come out with occasional bursts of anger. He or she will suffer from regular bouts of irritability and a short fuse.

Sometimes you see a person with three lines between the eyebrows. Three shallow lines indicate a liver problem, usually from too much frustration, anger, inappropriate diet, and alcohol. If the three lines are deep, the person is in danger of accidents. He or she is too yang—meaning too aggressive, single-mindedly focused, and stubborn. The person is usually so focused on what he or she is doing that he or she will be unable to hear the warnings from the universe as they come in the voices of others who urge the person to slow down or take stock. Usually, the warnings go unheeded.

Those with three lines should be careful. They have become too yang, too focused on achieving their goals. They need good yin—walks in a park or in nature; calming, peaceful music; aerobic exercise that stretches muscles and increases oxygen intake; and the company of loved ones. Such yin will help these people relax, enjoy life more, and open up to new ideas.

The person with a single line between the eyebrows presents an interesting set of issues. The single line usually emerges in a person with a strong constitution and a strong will. It may indicate more severe liver problems. In Japan, the single liver line is called "suspended needle," indicating danger. Many have this single line, and it often appears after some type of personal crisis, especially a mid-life crisis.

Those with liver problems indicated by this single line between the eyebrows should reduce their consumption of alcohol. They should avoid fatty foods, foods rich in sugar, chemical additives, and refined grains, like white rice. The liver cleanses the blood; the more polluted the blood, the more the liver must work to eliminate the toxins. If these poisons stay in the liver, they affect the organ's health and efficiency. The tiny blood vessels in the liver become hard, preventing blood and oxygen flow. Oriental medicine points out that leafy green vegetables, whole wheat and bulgur wheat, and small amounts of sour foods, such as sauerkraut and pickles, stimulate the liver, increase blood flow within it, and help restore health.

THE EYEBROWS

The popular theater in Japan is called Kabuki. The Kabuki actors come onstage dressed in garish costumes, with their faces painted wildly to exaggerate their characteristics. The good guys look very good; the bad guys have terrible, scary faces; the women are beautiful. The audience knows immediately whether a character is good or bad by his or her makeup—particularly the eyebrows, which tell whether each person is a good guy, a bad guy, or a fool.

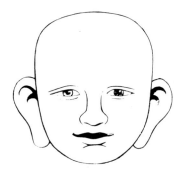

Draw in the eyebrows yourself and see how different eyebrows can change a face.

The fool, who is constantly in trouble, suffering many accidents of fate, is very funny-looking. He has eyebrows way up on his forehead and far apart, giving him the look of someone very unalert, or "spacey." His eyebrows reveal him as unintelligent, clownish, and accident-prone. The fool's eyes are usually round and *yin sanpaku,* meaning that the whites show on three sides, including below the iris. (I will explain more about sanpaku a little later in this chapter.)

The villain has very different eyebrows. His come sweeping down from the sides of his forehead to the top of his nose at a forty-five-degree angle, like two jets coming down on a target. There is very little space between the eyebrows over the nose; sometimes they are joined so as to become one long, frightening eyebrow. The villain's eyes are often *yang sanpaku,* with thick, dark makeup around them.

The hero has more balanced eyebrows, which rise and fall in a more gentle arc over his eyes. His eyebrows are long. His eyes are also more balanced, neither yin nor yang sanpaku.

The Kabuki theater uses the traditional wisdom of Oriental diagnosis to communicate with the audience in ways that are nonverbal, yet powerfully effective. Kabuki makeup is so effective because on some level, people know that one can detect characteristics in the face which reveal the inner nature, and that the eyebrows especially reveal that nature.

There are many types of eyebrows. Let's start with the basics.

Generally, the space between the eyebrows, above the nose, is about

One straight eyebrow clear across: a strong yang constitution, sometimes stubborn.

two fingers wide; when you bring together your index and middle fingers and place the tips in the space above your nose, the edges of your fingers should touch your eyebrows. This indicates a balanced constitution.

When the eyebrows are very close to each other over the nose or are joined, as if they were one eyebrow, it reveals a more yang constitution and disposition. The person whose brows look like this is more determined, more aggressive, more singularly focused. Such eyebrows appear in people whose mothers consumed more animal foods, especially animal proteins, when pregnant. Such people often focus narrowly on their own priorities, but they can also be extremely committed to a particular goal and work tirelessly to bring it to fruition. People with eyebrows that are close together or joined are enterprising. They are often ambitious and driven.

Eyebrows that are far apart—that is, more than two finger widths apart—indicate a more yin outlook on life. People with wide-set brows have a wide view of life, are curious, often sensuous, and want to experience much in life. People whose eyebrows are three fingers or more apart—a common trait, especially among celebrities and models— have great difficulty staying married to the same person. They are continually falling in love with some mysterious stranger.

People with eyebrows far apart are attracted to the arts, writing, and journalism. They need a profession that provides much change and variety. They do better with projects that have a limited duration, rather than the day-to-day plodding that business often demands.

Eyebrows not only tell personal characteristics, but also provide a clue about the state of a person's health during the course of his or her life. In Japan eyebrows were traditionally viewed in much the same

Thin eyebrows: a weak constitution.

Eyebrows are thick near the center of the face, thinner at the outer edges: born with a strong, healthy constitution but has a tendency to weaken the health through a poor life-style.

Strong bushy eyebrows at the outside edges, thin in the center: health is improving; the person has more and more life energy.

"Flying bird" eyebrows: health may change.

way as the lifeline on a person's palm: they were believed to reveal the length and quality of life.

It is important to note that eyebrows are only one sign in Oriental diagnosis, a single clue which must be added to many other clues before a sound judgment can be made. In other words, don't make your entire assessment on the eyebrows alone.

Sometimes you see eyebrows shaped like triangles or pennants, with the wide end at the edges of the face and the pointed end over the bridge of the nose, and getting thicker or bushier as they move to the periphery of the face. Such eyebrows indicate that the person's health was weak at birth but is gradually becoming stronger as he or she gets older.

Occasionally you see the opposite—eyebrows that are thick over the nose and thin at the periphery. The person with this sort of eyebrows was stronger at birth and in youth than he or she becomes later. Knowing this, such people should take better care of their health as they age.

Then there are people with "pushbroom" eyebrows—thick at both ends, the sort of eyebrows that Groucho Marx used to paint on his face. These people live such stable lives, with so few ups and downs and, therefore, so little movement, that you might say they were born so-so and will die so-so. They are the personification of stability.

Eyebrows that rise from the sides of the face to a high point over the nose—as if they were two sides of a mountain, forming a peak over the nose—suggest a more yin constitution and disposition. A person with such eyebrows has a gentle temperament and is not particularly ambitious. This person's attitude is "Live and let live." He or she is a peacemaker, someone who will go to great lengths to maintain harmony and avoid a fight.

Eyebrows that curve downward from the side of the face to the bridge of the nose suggest a far more aggressive personality. The person with such eyebrows is hard-driving, ambitious, and single-mindedly focused. When pushed, he or she fights back, and with a vengeance. This person is confrontational, seeing life as a struggle in which he or she often needs to fight for and win his or her goals. ABC newsman Sam Donaldson is a perfect example of a person with such eyebrows and such a disposition.

Eyebrows that go straight across the forehead suggest more balance, a person who is steady and experiences few ups and downs.

Eyebrows that rise and then sweep down toward the nose, forming a peak over each eye, suggest a personality with two extremes within. A person with brows like this can be hard-driving and ambitious, but also possesses a gentler side and a more poetic nature. This type of person must struggle through the first half of life to attain his or her goals. Eventually, however, this person reaches a point of balance and even peace at which he or she lives a more gentle existence, as revealed

Thick, bushy eyebrows, evenly wide: steady health, with radical changes unlikely.

by the downward sweep of the second half of the eyebrow. Such a person should guard his or her health during the second half of life, especially after fifty.

In the Orient, the eyebrows have long been associated with the intestines. In Oriental diagnosis, the life line on the palm—the long vertical line that arches from the base of the index finger to the bottom of the hand—reveals the inherited strength of the intestines. Oriental healers maintained that if your intestines are natively strong, you have a strong life line—and will live a long life. Since the eyebrows have also been associated with the relative strength of the intestines, the eyebrows, too, have been thought to indicate the length of a person's life.

No matter what their shape, consistently thick eyebrows are a sign of good health. Many people pluck their eyebrows because they have some notion that it makes them look better. It always strikes me as curious and revealing what people think of as beautiful. In any case, it is better not to pluck your eyebrows. The plucking of the eyebrows is an outward manifestation of an unconscious desire to eliminate some unhealthy accumulation of waste within the intestinal tract. Changing the diet to include more whole grains and fresh vegetables, which will increase the amount of fiber, will help eliminate the waste stored in the digestive system.

Slanted eyebrows, with large space between them: a yin condition, weak character.

Eyebrows that are sparse or thin suggest that the person should guard his or her health, avoiding extremes in diet and behavior, maintaining regular hours, and getting adequate exercise and rest. Often you see eyebrows that are thin at the ends; this means that the person will need to guard his or her health later in life.

Eyebrow hairs should all go in the same direction. Hairs that go in many directions indicate a life that goes in many directions. The person with eyebrows like this will make many changes, grow much, but be unable to stay with any particular course. Such people are changeable and undependable. They simply cannot make up their minds, and even when they do they doubt whether they have made the right decision, making real commitment impossible.

Occasionally you see eyebrows that grow in segments, that is, a section of hair grows in one direction, only to be interrupted by another section that grows in another direction. Sometimes you see several such segments, each one with hairs growing in different directions. This indicates that the person will experience several major changes in life; he or she will change careers, relationships, or residences, perhaps even moving to a foreign land for a time.

Both eyebrows slanted inward: a yang constitution.

Eyebrows that grow straight out from the head, like unruly hedges, indicate a person who is intelligent, nervous, and a bit neurotic. This type of person often reaches a position of power in society, especially in a scholarly or academic role. But such people can be irritable and impatient, especially with what they perceive as the limited intelligence or foibles of others.

Traditionally, eyebrows that are long and flow in one direction are regarded as the mark of a long and happy life. Such eyebrows ideally have a soft arc, sweeping gently up from the nose and turning downward at the edge of the face. They have a consistent thickness from start to finish, with long hairs at the end of the eyebrow. This type of person is usually relaxed, balanced, and more thoughtful.

THE EYES

Ten years ago Japanese food, especially sushi, was unknown in New York. Most people confronted by Japanese food thought it would be horrible to eat raw fish and rice. Now sushi is in fashion, and if you do not enjoy Japanese food you are thought to be out of step with the times.

Many people even prepare sushi and sashimi at home—and Japanese cookbooks have been turning up in kitchens all over the East and West coasts. Consequently, many people ask me, "Ohashi, when I shop for fish, how can I make sure it is fresh?" I tell them, "It's all in the eyes."

I enjoy shopping for fish. I have come to know how to tell fresh, healthy fish from unfresh fish, even when the fish salesman has tried to make the old fish look fresh. Now when the fish salesman sees me coming, he says, "Oh no, here comes that pain-in-the-butt Ohashi." The salesman knows that I know how to choose fish. Being Japanese, of course, I take a certain pride in this, because the Japanese are fishermen and we love fish. My wife is from Idaho. I never let her shop for fish. But she is very good when it comes to shopping for potatoes, of which I know nothing. We allow each other our specialties, and we are very happy, especially when we eat good fish and potatoes.

When you shop for fish, the first thing you should do is examine the eyes. A fresh fish has clear eyes that pop out. The eyes are convex and colored, usually blue; they should have a strong, healthy appearance. If the eyes are clouded, sunken, dull, or concave, don't buy that fish. It's not fresh.

Sometimes shrewd fish salesmen will cut off the head of the fish to fool you. In that case, check the gill to see if it is bright pink or red. That means the fish is fresh. A fresh fish, of course, does not smell fishy. It also has strong, firm scales. If the scales flake off easily, the fish is no good. Press your finger into the flesh; if it leaves an indentation, don't buy the fish. If the muscle responds quickly with resilience, the fish is fresh. But the eye of the fish will tell you most accurately how fresh the fish is.

It is the same way in Oriental diagnosis. I believe the eye provides

Fish: it's all in the eye.

sixty percent of the information you receive about a person's current condition.

Why does the eye reveal so much? First, the eye is directly connected to the brain via the optic nerve, and it will tell you the condition of the nervous system and the brain. When the nervous system or brain has been injured, the eye changes. At the very least, it loses clarity and alertness; at the worst, it may lose its ability to see.

Second, the brain requires thirty times more oxygen than other body cells. The eye requires eight times more oxygen than other body cells. Consequently, when the brain is receiving less oxygen than it needs, the first place that will be revealed is in the eyes, since the eyes are more sensitive to oxygen depletion than the rest of the body.

You know this from your own experience. Think back to the time when you sat in a crowded classroom or lecture hall listening to someone boring you to death. What happened? Your breathing became slow and shallow. The oxygen level to your brain diminished. Your eyes then became unbearably heavy. You were unable to concentrate, and your eyes were the first part of your body to react to your sleepiness after your brain.

When one is diagnosing another person's health or mental alertness, the eye is the most important tool in the body. No other organ can tell you as much about the person's inner condition. Let's take a closer look.

The first thing you will recognize about the eyes is their size, shape, and angle. Are the eyes round or narrow, large or small? Are they slanted up or down, or are they level?

Large, round eyes indicate a more yin constitution. The person with large, round eyes is a sensitive one. He or she is emotional and intuitive. Such a person will react adversely to stress. Large eyes indicate artistic talent; painters, writers, and other artists often have large eyes.

Large, round eyes often indicate a visionary, someone who sees the grand design of things, who perceives historical movements, political trends, or the changing patterns of opinion. Conversely, such people tend to neglect the details of projects. They see the direction in which a company or organization should head; they also see how that can be accomplished in principle, but they often overlook or neglect the details of carrying out such grand plans.

Small eyes indicate the ability to see and appreciate details. A small-eyed person will be one who likes to crunch numbers—an accountant or bookkeeper. Such a person has an affinity for the bottom line and wants to know how the grand design can be practically carried out. These people ask the down-to-earth questions. They are the perfect— indeed, the essential—complements to the visionaries. What the visionaries see, the practical people can carry out. But the people with small eyes usually cannot see the grand design. They are so immersed

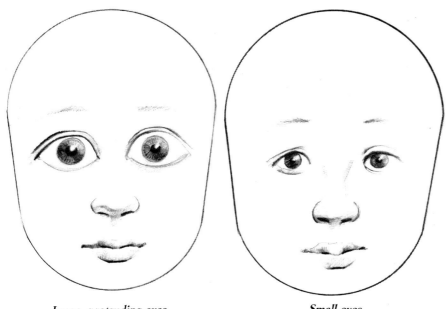

Large, protruding eyes.   *Small eyes.*

in the details of a project that they have trouble looking up and seeing the patterns in the sky. Therefore, they rarely have an overview of a project or of the direction of an organization.

Overall, round eyes indicate artistic talent. Large eyes indicate sensitivity and artistic talent. Small eyes reveal an attention to detail, focus, and a practical nature.

Small, round eyes show a strong, yang nervous system and an artistic talent that leads toward music. Such eyes reveal finger dexterity, coordination, and the type of mind that enjoys demanding tasks, such as the language of music. Musicians are often beautifully balanced between yin and yang, in that they appreciate the harmony, or wholeness, of music, as well as its nuances. Musicians must also have highly developed coordination and finger dexterity. They must translate the broad etheric vibrations of harmony into the hard realities of notes and sound.

The pianist Vladimir Horowitz is a perfect example of an artist with such eyes. His eyes were soft, round, small, and wise; they radiated with clarity and revealed a sparkling mind.

Next, you must look at a person's eyes to note whether they are level, or slanted upward or downward from the bridge of the nose.

Most slanting eyes slope downward from the edge of the face to the bridge of the nose. Such an angle reveals strong ambition. The greater the downward slant, the greater the ambition. Cartoons often depict evil people with eyes that have an extreme downward angle of this type; this extreme slant can reveal greed and megalomania. You must look at many eyes, however, before you can determine what a severe slant is. Many good and successful people have eyes with a downward

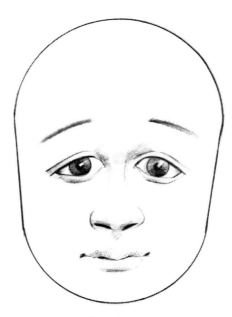

Slanted eyes.

slant that is not at all extreme and reveals no such negative characteristics.

Eyes that slope upward from the edge of the face to the bridge of the nose reveal a gentle, unambitious character. A person with such eyes is generally content with life. Such people don't push situations or people and prefer the path of least resistance. They are sensitive and often a bit timid. They prefer to give a little more to avoid conflict or struggle.

Eyes that are level, or straight across, reveal a balance between ambition and sensitivity. The person with level eyes has diplomatic skills. Such people can make fine negotiators because they can advance a particular point of view, understand the need for compromise, yet avoid giving away the farm.

Let's look at the position of the eye within the eye socket. When a baby is born, the iris, or colored part of the eye, is usually beautifully balanced between the upper and lower eyelids. It touches the upper and lower lids, so that no white, or sclera, shows above or below. The sclera is visible only to the left and right of the iris. This indicates a balanced and healthy nervous system. The baby is alert and in generally sound health.

When a person dies, the iris rises so that it partially disappears under the upper eyelid. The white sclera shows below. In the Orient, we call such an appearance *sanpaku,* which means "three whites" showing. Three whites, or sanpaku, is common among those who are ill or exhausted. It is most severe among those who are gravely ill and approaching death.

Three whites show that a person's nervous system is seriously imbalanced. Such a person's mind, body, and spirit are out of harmony with the larger forces of the cosmos. The person's intuition is off; his or her ability to assess people and situations is weak.

Generally, there are two types of sanpaku. The first is yin sanpaku, white showing below the iris, which is very common, especially among drug addicts. Here, the iris floats upward, revealing the sclera below. The second type is yang sanpaku, white showing above the iris; here the iris sinks downward toward the bottom eyelid. This reveals a dangerous or violent character. Charles Manson has beautiful yang sanpaku eyes.

If the white shows below the iris, the condition is yin, indicating that the danger comes from outside. A person with yin sanpaku eyes will place himself or herself in dangerous or threatening situations unwittingly—and may not survive.

If the white shows above, the condition is yang, and the danger comes from within. A person with yang sanpaku eyes is extremely violent, filled with rage, and likely poses a threat to himself and others. He may destroy himself, but may also take others with him.

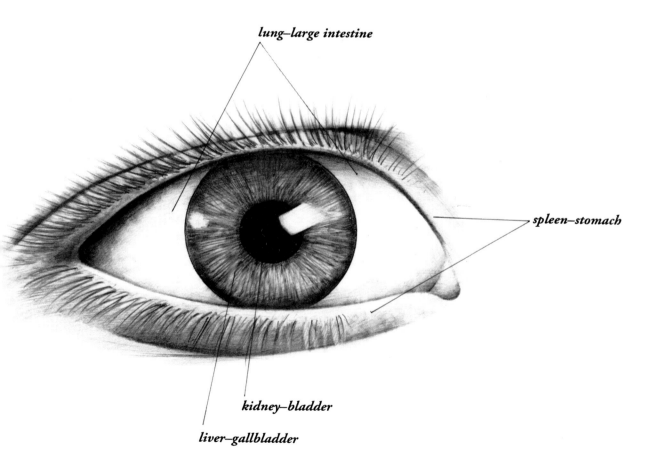

lung–large intestine

spleen–stomach

kidney–bladder

liver–gallbladder

Balanced, healthy eyes.

Yin sanpaku *eyes.*

Yang sanpaku *eyes.*

Protruding eye, or "surprise eye."

In Japan we call these "London-and-Paris eyes" because one looks to London, the other to Paris. They are also called dwelling eyes, or wandering eyes.

The macrobiotic philosopher George Ohsawa wrote a book called *You Are All Sanpaku* and dedicated it to John Kennedy and Abraham Lincoln, among others. Ohsawa said they were all seriously sanpaku and thus suffered from impaired judgment that indicated poor health and premature death. These people were excessively yin sanpaku. All of them accepted danger, but were unable to survive it.

Yin sanpaku, or white showing below the iris, is the result of excessive intake of yin substances, such as sugar, refined grains, alcohol, and medical drugs.

Yang sanpaku, or white showing above the iris, comes from excessive intake of meat, salt, and hard cheeses, and from indulgence in violence.

Cross-eyes: both eyes look toward the center.

One eye is centered; the other looks either outward (as in this illustration) or inward.

Yang sanpaku shows a character that is self-centered and bent on fulfilling its own ambitions, sometimes without regard for the cost.

Balanced eyes, with the iris touching the upper and lower lids, reveal a balanced condition and sound judgment. Balanced eyes come from a balanced view of life and sound dietary habits, especially the consumption of whole cereal grains and fresh vegetables.

When former Indian prime minister Indira Gandhi was killed, *Time* magazine published a series of photographs of her, including one taken just before she was assassinated. The picture clearly reveals her yin sanpaku eyes, which reflected her condition and revealed that she was in danger.

Sometimes the eyes of a person appear to cross or to look in two directions. When the right eye looks right and the left looks left, we Japanese call it "London-and-Paris eyes"—one eye looks at London while the other looks at Paris. This reveals a serious yin imbalance in the nervous system—too many liquids, sugar, alcohol, and drugs. The person with such eyes has a tendency to develop diabetes and disorders of the nervous system. These people are accident-prone; they are the victims of accidents, rather than the causes of them. Accidents happen to these people because their eyes are out of balance. These people also have great difficulty in making decisions. They cannot see their direction clearly and are torn between two paths, just as their eyes look in two directions.

Eyes that are crossed when relaxed reveal problems of the nervous system, liver, and heart. The cause is too many yang foods, such as meat, hard cheeses, and salt, and deep psychological conflict within. People with crossed eyes will cause accidents because they have limited vision. Also their eyes reveal an inner conflict: two sides of their body and mind are at war. That conflict manifests itself in daily phenomena. You should ask such a person whether his or her parents got along, or whether there was an extreme imbalance in the family. Was one of the parents ill? Were both parents extremely willful and uncompromising? Crossed eyes also reveal a frustration with being unable to settle conflicts to one's satisfaction.

What if a person is born with this condition? It is possible that the cervical or neck bones may have been damaged during delivery as they were born, causing this problem. Or perhaps the person's mother ate many strong yang foods during her pregnancy.

Sometimes one eye looks straight ahead, while the other drifts to the periphery. If the left eye drifts, the problem is too many sweet substances, such as sugar and refined grains, alcohol, and drugs. If the right eye drifts, the problem is too much animal food, such as meat, hard cheeses, and poultry. I have found many cancer patients with eyes like this. (See "General Dietary Guidelines" in chapter 9 for suggestions on ways of achieving balance and harmony in daily eating.)

THE EYE BAGS

Just below the eye is a small pouch, or eye bag, that is often swollen or dark. Whenever a person shows darkness or swollen pouches below the eyes, people say the person needs more sleep. This bit of folk wisdom is correct in the view of Oriental diagnosis. But there is a great deal more to say about this area of the face.

This area has the highest water content of any part of the face. At the same time, the skin here is thinnest, without oil glands, making the area very responsive to changes in the body's water content. This, combined with the careful observations of healers through the ages, is the reason that traditional Oriental diagnosticians regard the area under the eyes as the place that reveals the condition of the kidneys.

In the Orient, the kidneys are highly revered organs. They are viewed in abstract as well as concrete terms. Traditional healers see the kidneys as the storehouse of ki, or the life force. The kidneys distribute ki to the rest of the body, maintaining the vitality inherent in a person's constitution.

For this reason, it is said that the kidneys are the vaults in which the inheritance of the ancestors is stored. This means that the kidneys reveal the wealth of your genetic lineage. (I will have a great deal more to say about the kidneys when I discuss the ears, which reveal the constitution of the kidneys. Now I am talking strictly about the condition of the kidneys, as revealed below the eyes.)

The kidneys purify the blood by removing waste. These organs, therefore, take on an abstract meaning: they separate the necessary things in life from the unnecessary. The kidneys have the important function of helping us distinguish what is valuable in our experience from what is unnecessary and to be discarded.

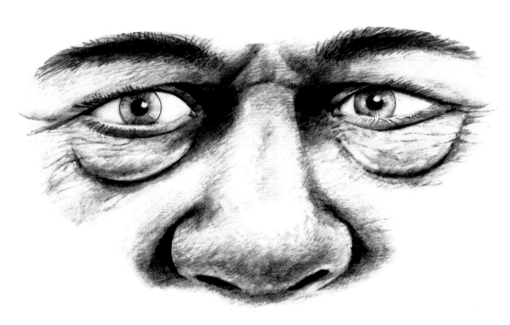

Bags under the eyes: kidney weakness. This is becoming increasingly common.

The condition of our kidneys plays a large role in our overall health. If a person feels weak or chronically tired, he or she should rest and treat the kidneys.

There are three ways in which we can harm our kidneys. The first is by living against the rhythms of nature. People do this who work at night and sleep during the day, such as nurses, night-shift factory workers, thieves, and people who travel extensively, especially to places more than one time zone from home. (I will explain this in greater detail shortly.)

The second way in which we can damage our kidneys is by draining ourselves of energy. People do this who work too hard, especially at jobs they do not enjoy. Another way of expending too much energy is by indulging in too much sex.

The third way in which we can harm our kidneys is by poor diet, especially by eating foods out of season, such as watermelon in winter, or by eating highly refined foods or those with many chemical additives.

Living Against Nature

Since the kidneys are responsible for the flow of ki throughout the body, they must be protected to ensure overall health. Severe disruptions in routine—such as working during the hours when the body has grown accustomed to resting, and resting during the hours when we are used to working—throw off the body's cycles. These cycles were not established during our lifetimes, but are part of human evolution. Since the birth of humans on the planet, we and our ancestors have been rising with the sun and sleeping with the stars. We have been conditioned to follow this same pattern since we were born. Biological systems have developed in accordance with these cycles—vitamin D metabolism and many hormonal functions, for example. We cannot change it as simply as we might think. When we live in opposition to the natural cycles, we exhaust and ultimately injure our kidneys.

The area below the eye, or eye bag, darkens whenever we drain our natural reserves of ki from the kidneys. People who work at night and sleep during the day are an example of those who are exhausting their natural strength. People who stay out late at night and sleep during the day are the same.

Those who work for the airlines or fly regularly on business also violate natural cycles and harm the kidneys. Travel to different time zones upsets the body's natural rhythms. Day and night become confused; sleeping and waking cycles are disturbed. Moreover, long flights to different climates affect metabolism and daily eating habits. We can fly from the cold winter weather of New York City, for example, to the sunny climate of Southern California in a few hours. Our bodies must adjust to the sudden change. On such a trip, we may also eat different food—more tropical dishes, fruit, and light cooking. All of this has an incredible impact on our metabolism, especially on our kidneys and adrenal glands.

I believe it is essential to protect the kidneys when traveling, and I recommend the following precautionary measures:

1. As often as you can, travel with the sun. This is not always possible, of course, but it is far easier on the body to go with nature than against it. Traveling against the sun puts us immediately in a different time zone and shortens the day more rapidly. For every

change of time zone, the body needs at least one day to recover. A two-hour change requires two days to adapt and reestablish the body's rhythms.

2. Bring your own food, preferably natural food, such as brown rice or some other grain, or the food with which your body is acquainted. Such food is easier on digestion. If you cannot bring your own food, select food that grows in your home climate. This will make less severe demands on your body as it adjusts to your new location.

   Try to eat the foods that are easiest to digest, such as whole grains, fresh vegetables, beans, and fish. Avoid foods that are hard on digestion, such as red meat, hard cheeses, and baked goods, and avoid excessively refined foods that contain large amounts of white sugar or alcohol.

3. Don't drink alcohol before departure or on an airplane. Because of the altitude, alcohol has three times the effect on the body that it has on the ground: one beer at thirty-five thousand feet equals three beers at sea level. The alcohol gets into the bloodstream faster and has an almost instantaneous effect on brain chemistry.

4. As much as possible, stay with your home time. When you cross time zones, your body must make two major readjustments—once going and once coming. If you must cross time zones, go to sleep as close to your normal sleeping hour and wake as close to your normal time as you can.

Whenever we drink too much liquid, the area below the eyes becomes swollen. Excessive consumption of liquids overworks the kidneys, and as they become tired, the area below the eyes becomes increasingly dark. The system is showing fatigue. The kidneys need rest and less liquid.

Many healthy authorities admonish us to drink as many as eight glasses of water per day. This is misguided, in my opinion. It is the result of our modern, imbalanced diet. The kidneys and the overall system would not have to be flushed out if we were not consuming so many chemical toxins in refined foods, and so much fat and cholesterol. A diet composed of whole grains, fresh vegetables, beans, sea vegetables (such as *nori, wakame,* and *konbu*), and fish—in short, the diet humans evolved on—provides optimal nutrition without the chemical toxins and excessive fats that need to be washed from the system.

We have been blessed with many healthy urges, two of which—hunger and thirst—have guided us quite nicely through evolution. Before this century, there were no healthy authorities to advise people that they should drink eight glasses of water per day. People drank when thirsty, and got all the liquid they needed.

Each person's system is different. The amount of water we take in depends so much on our life-style, the kind of work we do, the amount of salt we consume, the season of the year, and the place where we live. For example, if you live near the ocean, your pores tend to absorb more sodium from the sea. Consequently, you naturally desire more water. If you work on a farm and sweat profusely, you will also desire more water. But if you work in an air-conditioned office building, your water requirements may be different. There is no single standard that can be applied uniformly. However, we can trust our bodies. Thirst has been working for aeons, and I feel confident that it is still the best guide for determining the amount of liquid we consume.

Another way in which we can harm the kidneys through drinking is to consume excessively cold drinks. This shocks the body, especially the kidneys, and causes them to function poorly.

Sometimes you see small pimples beneath the eye. These show that there is too much mucus within the tiny renal arteries that make up the kidney. The presence of kidney stones can be seen in the form of hard pimples or dark dots in the pouches below the eye. Excessive consumption of fats and cholesterol contributes to the formation of kidney stones.

Often you see that the area below the eye is darkened, brown, or even black. As the area becomes increasingly dark, the person approaches severe illness and even death. The kidneys are becoming exhausted. They are unable to purify the blood. Consequently, waste is building up within the kidneys and in the blood.

Excessive salt consumption also shows up as darkness in the eye bags. Consuming too much salt harms the kidneys and causes high blood pressure. Salt creates contraction, forcing the tiny renal arteries to close. This has the same effect as pinching a garden hose: the liquid backs up and pressure builds behind the pinched area.

The kidneys are regarded as the seat of sexual vitality. However, by engaging in sex excessively, a person can exhaust and damage the kidneys. This is especially true for men. Excessive sex is a personal standard, of course. Its definition is guided by the individual's constitution, physical health, psychological needs, and current diet. Ancient Taoist masters provided the following guideline in such matters: men in their twenties should allow at least two days of rest between sexual encounters; men in their thirties should allow three days of rest; men in their forties should allow four days, and so on.

Whether you wish to follow this guideline is strictly up to you. However, if you begin to see darkness or swelling below your eye during times when you are enjoying a great abundance of sex, perhaps you should consider slowing down and giving your body a rest, at least until your eye bags disappear.

Excess stress also damages the kidneys. Stress adversely affects the adrenal glands, which pump adrenaline into the bloodstream, keeping us in a state of alertness and fear. Continual fear and stress break down the kidneys and can eventually lead to death.

Women who have had abortions usually suffer some type of very subtle kidney damage because of the shock to the system caused by the abortion. Therefore, careful diet—especially the avoidance of fatty and oily foods—and adequate rest after the abortion are vital to recovery of the kidney and the restoration of the female sex organs.

Children should not have eye bags or darkness below the eyes. When a child does show eye bags or darkness, his or her kidneys should be well cared for. Longer hours of sleep should be enforced, and the kidney area should be kept warm to allow better blood circulation. If a mother is breast-feeding, she should avoid cigarette smoking, all drugs, and alcohol.

The body is our vehicle for experience and spiritual growth while we sojourn here on the earth. As we come to understand the workings of the body, mind, and spirit, our ability to sustain and promote our health is enhanced. Our understanding of life grows as well. Therefore, understanding and protecting the body are acts of spiritual mastery.

THE NOSE

The Bridge of the Nose

The bridge of the nose corresponds to the spine. Often you see a person whose nose is turned either toward the left or toward the right side of the face. This common trait indicates that the spine is not straight: there is a bend, or scoliosis, either to the left or to the right, often in the same direction the nose takes.

The muscles in the back, shoulders, neck, and face are all intimately connected. If there is stress on one side of the body, which is often the cause of some spinal aberration, all the muscles in the back, neck, and face compensate for this stress. Imbalances in the back are often reflected in our posture, the way we hold our shoulders, our necks, and our faces.

When the muscles in the face are affected by stress, the features naturally change. Stress can create mild to severe abnormalities. The face turns this way or that because the muscles on one side are pulled by the imbalance in the spine. When the imbalance in the spine is severe enough, the muscles pull the nose in one direction or the other. When the spine is straight, the nose is straight. Often proper exercises and Ohashiatsu can do much to correct such an imbalance.

The Nose Itself

In Oriental diagnosis, the round end of the nose has long been associated with the condition of the heart. The nostrils reveal the constitutional strength of the lungs.

Right and left nostrils are both large and of equal size.

The connection between the nostrils and the lungs is obvious. The nostrils are the gateway for oxygen to the lungs and are therefore one with the respiratory system. Wide, flaring nostrils reveal large lungs with great oxygen capacity. Large lungs are a sign of strength and the potential for success in life. Lungs are more than mere sacks of air; they represent the body's ability to take in the life force—ki—which animates a person throughout life. If an individual's ability to take in life is small, that person's potential to give out—to create, to impress his or her vision on life—is equally small. However, if the potential to take in ki is great, a person's potential to affect life along the lines of his or her ambition is also great.

Sometimes you see nostrils of different sizes in the same nose. The left nostril is small, while the right is large, or vice versa. This indicates that the lungs are of different sizes as well. The small nostril will correspond to the small lung, the large nostril to the large lung.

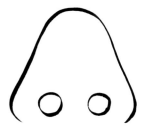

Big nose but small nostrils.

In the groove where the nostril meets the face, the condition of the bronchi can be seen. This area becomes red and inflamed from the overconsumption of dairy products, sugar, and food with chemical additives. This reddening means that the bronchi are becoming congested with mucus. The suggested remedies are a change in diet, especially an increase in the consumption of leafy green vegetables; plenty of fresh air; and adequate rest.

The basis for much of Oriental medicine is founded on the principle that deep channels of energy run in orderly patterns throughout the body. These channels, called meridians, nourish specific systems in the body, though they often travel significant distances from the organ systems they nourish. Several meridians, for example, run through the head region, including the meridians that nourish the bladder, gallbladder, stomach, and small and large intestines. The large-intestine meridian (one on each side of the body) begins at the tip of the index finger and ends at the tip of the nose, right below the nostril.

When the large intestine cannot adequately eliminate, the energy moves upward along the meridian to the nose and sinuses. This results in mucus and congestion in the sinuses, causing mucous discharge, headaches, and other discomforts.

Left nostril is smaller than the right.

Since the nose and sinuses are part of the respiratory system, the lungs also become congested when the large intestine cannot eliminate. One of the ways we treat the common cold, therefore—or any sinus or lung problem—is to treat the large intestine. When stagnation is eliminated there, the sinuses open and the lungs begin to clear.

It is common knowledge that the noses of alcoholics become red and lined with broken capillaries—so common that it's a mystery why more people do not make this simple connection: that alcohol, a very yin substance, causes capillaries to expand in the nose and elsewhere on the face. This is a very easily observed example of how the internal condition is reflected in the face.

The condition of the heart can be seen in the nose. The nose has two distinct muscles within it which should come together during gestation. Often you see a cleft in the nose, either at the bottom or in the middle. This means that the left and right sides of the heart are not well coordinated. The person with such a cleft may have a mild heart murmur, or may have had a murmur in childhood.

The more pronounced the cleft, the more serious the heart condition. This can be remedied by making appropriate changes in diet and lifestyle, reducing the consumption of fat and cholesterol and eliminating excess stress.

The heart is an electrical pump. The electricity that runs the pump is the product of an oxygen-ionization process. Oxygen molecules lose an electron, causing electrons to flow along a circuit in the heart, and this flow of electricity causes the heart to beat. The oxygen is provided by three coronary arteries that carry blood to the heart muscle. Often the three coronary arteries are clogged with plaque, a condition called arteriosclerosis. This condition is caused by a diet rich in fat and cholesterol. The plaque builds up inside the arteries leading to the heart, closing each one off at a different rate. This allows different amounts of oxygen to get to the heart, creating an imbalance that causes the electrical circuit around the heart to become uncoordinated and spastic. This impairment of the electrical circuit causes the heart to beat irregularly, and ultimately can result in a heart attack.

Such a problem can readily be seen on a person's face. When the heart is strained and suffocating for lack of oxygen, capillaries in the face begin to expand. The face becomes red. The nose becomes red and swollen. Sometimes red vessels appear in the bulb of the nose. A person whose face looks this way is very close to a heart attack and should consult a physician immediately.

Occasionally you see a person who has hair growing out of the nostrils. This indicates that the person is consuming a great deal of animal protein. His or her coronary arteries are loaded with fat and cholesterol from animal food.

You may also notice people with noses that are pale but swollen.

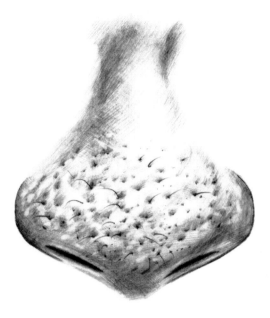

Enlarged and swollen nose with red spots and hairs: a heart weakened by overconsumption of alcohol.

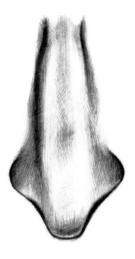

Pointed, red, and thin nose: difficulty in breathing.

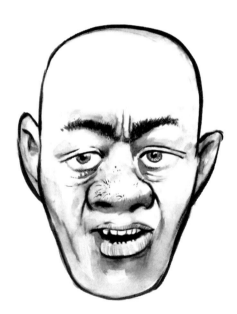

Broken skin on nose, yin sanpaku eyes, and lines between the eyebrows: heart and liver problems due to excess consumption of alcohol and drugs.

This suggests a heart swollen from too much dairy food—also rich in fat and cholesterol—and perhaps from too much caffeine.

The Chinese regarded the entire nose, including the bridge, as the diagnostic tool for the pancreas and spleen. If a person's nose or bridge is red, it indicates the presence of hypoglycemia. The cause is too much sugar, fruit, and fruit juice.

THE PHILTRUM

Below the nose is the small vertical cleft called the philtrum. This cleft is formed by the powerful fusing of the face during gestation. When we are inside the womb, our development recapitulates human evolution; during much of our gestation, we resemble fish, with eyes on each side of our heads and mouths wide across the entire bottom of our faces. Gradually the face closes, the result of a powerful yang force. The eyes come to the front of the face; the nose fuses; the mouth becomes smaller; and the philtrum is formed, serving as a reminder of the powerful forces that brought us into being.

If the yang force during gestation was strong, the philtrum is deep, clear, and sharp. If the yang force was weaker, the philtrum is shallower and lighter.

A clear yang philtrum indicates deep constitutional strength. People with yang philtra are often ambitious, focused, and goal-oriented. They often have strong appetites for life, especially for food and sex. These appetites are even more pronounced when the distance between the nose and upper lip is long.

People with light or shallow philtra have more yin constitutions. They prefer to work with their minds rather than their bodies; they are gentler. They are not as sexually motivated as those with strong philtra, though sex is still an important area of their lives. They will parcel out their energies, their life force, to achieve their more important goals. They are simply not driven by overwhelming energy, as are those with prominent philtra and strong yang constitutions.

Besides being deep or shallow, the philtrum can have a variety of shapes. For most people, especially for those with strong, clear philtra, the shape is bounded by two parallel lines. Sometimes you see the two lines flare out at an angle from each other, like the sides of an upside-down triangle that do not meet. A person with such a philtrum was born weak but will gradually gain strength through life and will experience an improvement in health as he or she grows older. If the triangle is right-side-up, the reverse is true. Such a person was born strong and will gradually weaken.

Occasionally you see the two sides of the philtrum shaped like bows turned in opposite directions, forming an oval. This means that at the beginning of life, this person's health was weak; the person will ex-

PHILTRUM LINES

Lines are parallel.

Space is narrow at the top, wide at the bottom.

Space between lines is wide at the top, narrow at the bottom.

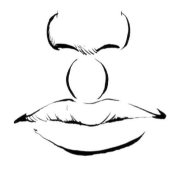

The top is narrow; space widens, then becomes narrow again.

No philtrum lines.

perience improved health during the middle years, but on reaching old age must guard his or her health because it becomes more sensitive.

Often you see women with mustaches. Because the area above the upper lip corresponds with the sex organs, a mustache on a woman means that the sex organs are troubled. Usually the problem is that the sex organs are clogged with too much mucus and protein, which cannot be fully eliminated during menstruation. Young women with mustaches very often have trouble becoming pregnant. Generally conception occurs, but implantation of the fertilized egg is hampered. The uterus and the egg itself are coated with mucus, making implantation difficult, if not impossible.

Women with hair on their chins are suffering from hormonal imbalances, usually from consuming too much fatty food and from overeating. Fat causes hormone imbalances in both men and women, and its consumption should be kept to a minimum, especially if a person is experiencing any hormonal problem.

THE MOUTH

The digestive tract begins, obviously, at the mouth and ends at the anus. It is essentially a long tube that assimilates food into the bloodstream and the cells of the body. In my classes, I like to make a drawing of a person shaped like a soda can, with a tube running from an opening at one end of the can to another opening at the other end. The drawing

OHASHI'S IMAGINARY HUMAN

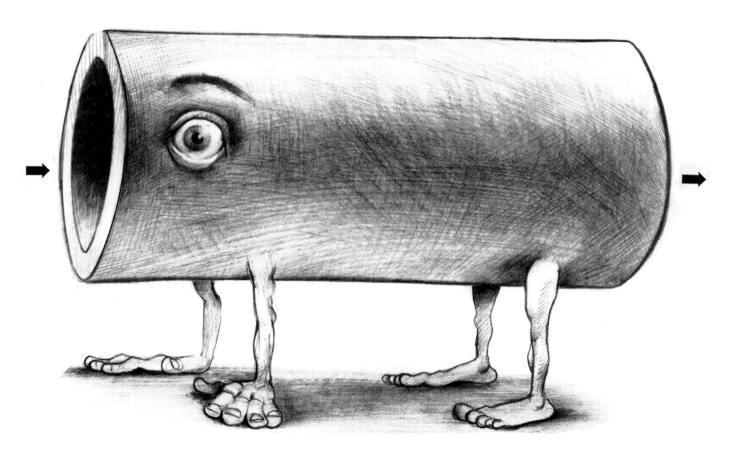

Materials go in. Leftover materials go out.

reveals the essential oneness of the digestive tract and the unity between one end and the other. It is important to understand this unity to fully appreciate how to diagnose the intestines.

The intestines are constantly taking in food from the environment and eliminating waste, which goes back to the environment. This exchange is similar to the workings of the lung, which takes in oxygen—another essential element of life—from the environment and eliminates waste in the form of carbon dioxide. For this reason, Oriental healers have long regarded the large intestine and the lungs as related organs. (I will have a lot more to say about related organs in chapter 3, when I discuss the theory of the Five Elements or Five Transformations.)

In traditional Japan, people said that the mouth should be no wider than the nose, but I teach my students that the normal width of a mouth equals the distance between the pupils of the eyes. If you draw two imaginary lines directly downward from the pupils, the edges of the mouth should fall inside the lines.

Mouths that are wider than these lines reveal a more yin or expanded intestinal tract. People with wide mouths suffer from digestive trouble, either chronic diarrhea or constipation. If the lips of a wide mouth are often wet, usually the person suffers from chronic diarrhea; if the mouth is chronically dry, constipation is indicated.

The lips should be full but tight. They should have a nice curve, and should not appear swollen or distended.

Occasionally, swollen lips mean that peristalsis and nutrient assimilation are weak. People with tight or narrow lips usually eat excessive amounts of beef and other red meat. The intestines of such people are clogged with uneliminated waste. You see this tightness often in the top lips of older Americans. Nutrient assimilation is hampered, and degeneration is taking place.

The upper lip reveals the condition of the stomach and small intestine. It also shows the strength of the appetite.

The top of the upper lip, where the red lip meets the skin, reveals the condition of the stomach. If the lip is well defined, the stomach is natively strong. If the red lip is obscured where it meets the skin, the stomach is not as strong and should be protected.

The bottom of the upper lip reveals the state of the small intestine. Often you see white patches here; they reveal a lack of circulation in the small intestine. If the patches are dark red or purplish, there is serious blood stagnation, and remedial measures should be taken: a change in diet, exercise (especially exercises that stretch the midsection of the body), Ohashiatsu, and perhaps acupuncture.

The bottom lip reveals the condition of the large intestine and colon. It also shows the strength of food assimilation.

The bottom lip, too, should be full and well shaped. Often you see a person whose bottom lip is swollen, indicating chronic bowel prob-

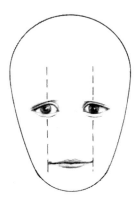

Parallel lines drawn vertically through the center of the pupils should touch the ends of the mouth. If the ends extend farther, then this person has "Big Mouth."

Healthy lips, evenly developed, wet, with nice color.

Upper and lower lips are the same size.

Upper lip is thicker and dominates.

Lower lip is thicker and dominates.

lems. Peristalsis is weak, and the person suffers from diarrhea or constipation. Check the bottom lip for red or brown dots, indicating ulcers or hemorrhoids. The person usually suffers from hemorrhoids if the lower lip is particularly swollen and heavily lined.

Swollenness, of course, is a relative quality. Check the lips to see if a particular side or part is swollen.

The corners of the mouth reveal the condition of the duodenum. Often people suffer from sores in the corners of the mouth. This is the result of too much fat in the diet, which builds up within the duodenum and causes the liver and gallbladder to secrete greater quantities of bile acids. Bile acids are necessary to break down fat. However, the more bile acids secreted, the harsher and more toxic the intestinal environment. Numerous scientific studies have shown that excessive bile acid secretion causes carcinogens to become more powerful and trigger tumor growth.

For good digestion, chewing is essential. A mouthful of food should be chewed thirty-five to fifty times. The more we chew, the more we secrete saliva, which is essential to healthy digestion. Saliva contains needed enzymes that begin the digestion process. It is also highly alkaline, which prepares food for the stomach and intestines. Once food enters the stomach and duodenum, acid secretion takes place. The alkaline-based food balances the acidic environment of the stomach, protecting the stomach from excess acid that would otherwise give rise to stomach disorders, including ulcers. If we fail to chew our food adequately, the stomach environment has no alkaline buffer to balance its powerful acids. These acids act on the stomach lining and cause a host of stomach and digestive illnesses.

Besides chewing well, it is best not to drink while you eat, or immediately after you eat. The more you drink, the more you wash away the saliva within your mouth.

Every nationality has its gifts and peculiarities when it comes to eating. I like to tell my students the Japanese eat with their eyes: everything has to be beautiful before they are willing to put the food in their mouths. The Chinese eat with their noses: the food must smell good before they will touch it. Also, they have to smell it a mile away before their appetites are whetted. The Italians and French eat with their tongues: the food must be very rich; there must be lots of sauces and an enormous variety of flavors.

The Americans eat with their "guts." They also like to "eat and run." All over the country, I see signs saying "eat and run," or "fast food," or "food to go." But, I ask myself, who wants to eat and run? It's not good for you.

Don't eat and run. Eat and relax; chew well, and protect your digestion and your life. The more you enjoy your eating, the more you will enjoy your life.

THE TEETH

Many secrets about life are revealed in the teeth. The teeth show us what our mothers ate, especially during the nine months they carried us. The teeth also tell us much about our relationships with our mothers and about our upbringing. They tell us the diet of our ancestors, and the foods we should eat to maintain health and direction in life. Finally, the teeth have an important and interesting relationship with the spine, about which I will talk more later.

Let's begin at the beginning—the very beginning—when sperm and egg meet and form a living fetus. Sperm and egg are two cells that combine to form the full complement of genes and a living human embryo. At this point, the cells begin to divide rapidly, and fetal growth takes place.

In my classes, I like to make a drawing of these two cells—sperm and egg—combining; the two become one. But the evidence of the two cells remains everywhere in our bodies as the duality of life. One aspect of that duality is the formation of teeth and vertebrae. Teeth and vertebrae are two sets of small bones—one set smaller than the other, yes, but still very much alike.

There are thirty-two teeth, and thirty-two vertebrae. During gestation, one set of small bones moves upward to the mouth to form the teeth; the other moves downward to form the spine. The relationship between the teeth and the vertebrae continues through life. Our ability to chew, for example, depends on the straightness of the spine. If the spine becomes crooked or impaired in some way, chewing is impaired; we may develop an underbite or overbite. The jaw can become imbalanced to one side or the other, so that one side of the mouth bites before the other does. It can be very painful to chew at all if there is a misalignment of the spine. Tension in the back is often expressed by gritting the teeth or clenching the jaw; the jaw often tries to release the tension that accumulates in the spine.

When I discuss the spine in greater depth in chapter 5, we will see this complementary relationship between the jaw and the spine.

All of our teeth, including our adult teeth, are formed during gestation. They are all present within the upper gums when we are born. Teeth are made of calcium and other minerals. Like the rest of our constitution, their strength depends on our mother's diet. We will have teeth no matter what our mothers ate, but the strength of those teeth depends on the availability of calcium, phosphorous, magnesium, and other nutrients from our mother's diet.

What the mother eats reveals a great deal about her attitude toward pregnancy and her child. If the mother eats a lot of fruit and sugar and drinks alcohol or takes drugs, the child's teeth will be weak. Often this type of diet during pregnancy reveals a mother in conflict over her pregnancy. She seeks to escape her reality by using these foods and other substances.

This conflict can cause disturbances in the mother's flow of ki. Energies accumulate in certain organs, such as the liver, where anger and hostility can become trapped. These energies do not run smoothly throughout the body, failing to nourish other parts of the mother's body and the fetus. The more conflict in the mother's life, the more she is attracted to foods that will weaken her and her baby. These factors—the mother's diet, her attitudes during pregnancy, and the support of her external environment, namely her partner—all combine to enhance or diminish the strength of the child's constitution, including his or her teeth.

Crooked teeth in a child are a sign of some type of difficulty for the mother during pregnancy. The energies that governed the straight descent of the teeth were not stable but in conflict, causing the teeth themselves to be in conflict with one another.

Buck teeth reveal that the mother consumed a lot of salad and raw vegetables, fruit, fruit juice, and sugar during pregnancy. Teeth that jut forward are caused by such yin, or expansive, foods.

Teeth that slant back, like those of a shark, reveal an overly yang diet during pregnancy, including such foods as red meat, eggs, chicken, and salt.

Good, strong teeth during childhood and adulthood reveal a functional family that was conscious of the need to take care of the child, including his or her teeth. The family ate a healthful diet rich in fresh vegetables. Vegetables, of course, are the source of many vitamins and minerals essential to healthy teeth.

Teeth that are weak or suffer from cavities reveal that the mother's diet during pregnancy lacked minerals, weakening her own condition. Later development of cavities indicates a family that did not pay much attention to dental hygiene and early dietary patterns. Refined foods, especially sugars, cause the mouth and blood to become rich in acid, which causes tooth decay. Acid-rich blood is a host for many viruses and colds, causing poor health in children.

A child will, of course, affect his or her own teeth by the way he or she eats. If a child's training is good and dietary habits sound, his or her teeth will develop well. If, however, a child is in conflict or suffers a painful childhood, he or she will be attracted to more yin foods to escape consciousness and encourage a fantasy existence. Such substances as sugar, soda pop, excess fruit, fruit juice, and refined flour facilitate the creation of a fantasy world to compensate for difficulties and pain in the immediate environment.

• • •

Teeth reveal many secrets of human evolution. Paleontologists study fossilized teeth to learn the diets of our forebears. Let's see what we can learn about our evolution and the diet it has designed for us.

We possess thirty-two teeth, which can be broken down as follows: four canine, or sharp, pointed teeth; eight incisors, or front teeth; twenty molars and premolars.

Canine teeth are used for tearing meat. If you look into the mouth of a lion or tiger—animals whose principal food is meat—you will see a mouthful of canine teeth. The same is true for dogs and cats. These animals also have very short digestive tracts. Their teeth and their intestines are perfect for the consumption of meat, which requires sharp, pointed teeth to tear animal flesh, and digestive tracts that are short so that the animal food can be eliminated quickly. The longer meat remains in the intestines, the more likely it is to putrefy and cause disease. Evolution has equipped these animals well for their specific eating habits.

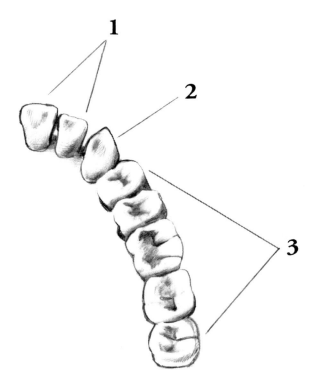

Human teeth: (1) incisors for cutting vegetables and fruits; (2) canine for tearing meat or fish; (3) molars for grinding grains. In terms of our teeth, we humans should eat two portions of vegetables and five portions of grain for every one portion of meat in our diet.

Cows have no canine teeth, only incisors and molars, which indicates that their diets are made entirely of vegetable matter, in this case grass and grains. Incisors are long, wide, and flat at the bottom, like the cutting edge of a vegetable knife. They bite down and cut. Vegetables and fruits are most amenable to such teeth. Incisors bite off food; they do not grind or process it into smaller bits in the mouth.

The primary function of molars, which do the bulk of the work, is grinding. The foods molars work best with are grains and, to a lesser extent, vegetables. Anyone who has ever tried to eat a piece of steak knows that the meat cannot be fully masticated by the molars and must be swallowed whole; it goes down as a wad of sinew. Since the intestines have no teeth, they are not well equipped to deal with this lump. Consequently, much of the animal food we eat is never fully digested, and a percentage of it is not even eliminated from the bowels. It remains there in pockets to decay, sometimes causing serious illness, including colon cancer.

Those who eat meat regularly have higher levels of ammonia in their blood and tissues. The excess protein in meat breaks down into nitrogen, which forms ammonia. Ammonia is one of the most powerful and destructive toxins in the body. It deforms cells and DNA and can cause cancer. Ammonia also smells bad. It is ammonia that gives rise to body odor and the enormous deodorant industry.

Grains and vegetables, on the other hand, can be fully masticated; they are ground up into tiny bits that can be further digested in the stomach and intestines. Grains and vegetables also have the added benefit of fiber, which cleans the intestines of waste. Fiber moves waste along the intestinal tract and helps eliminate it from our bodies.

The ideal ratio of grains to vegetables to animal foods in the human diet is 5:2:1. Evolution has predisposed us to eating a diet composed of five parts grains, two parts vegetables, and one part animal or protein foods.

This, essentially, is the diet of most traditional peoples. No matter where you look in the world, you see the same general diet, whether it is in Asia, Europe, Africa, India, the Middle East, or among the American Indians. In Asia, the grains are brown rice, barley, millet, and wheat; in Europe, wheat, barley, millet, and oats; in Africa, millet and wheat; in India and the Middle East, mostly wheat; among the Indians of America, especially South and Central America, mostly corn.

Historically, humans have eaten all sorts of animal foods. However, the amounts were limited and were eaten with grains and vegetables. Generally, consumption of animal foods was restricted to feasts and holidays because supplies of animal food, especially of beef and pork were limited. Also, it has been universally understood by traditional peoples that eating grains and vegetables brings longevity and that the consumption of animal foods should be restricted to maintain health.

As I have said, teeth and digestion are intimately linked. The Japanese, for example, have long been eaters of grains, principally rice. Consequently the Japanese have a much longer digestive tract than many Western peoples, especially those whose consumption of animal foods has increased over the past few generations.

The appearance of teeth in babies tells us about the development of their digestion as well. The first teeth to emerge in a baby's mouth are usually incisors. Their emergence indicates that the baby is ready for some vegetable broth. The development of the digestive system is still limited; whole foods cannot yet be consumed, as indicated by the absence of the molars necessary to grind the food. As the molars come in, the parents can increase the amount of whole foods in the baby's diet. The first whole food should be a very wet grain porridge.

As the baby develops a mouthful of teeth, it is ready to be weaned and given more whole foods. Salt consumption should be limited in infants and children, of course. Vegetables should be cooked without salt for young children, and salt should be introduced in limited quantities as the child passes the age of five.

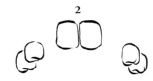

Incisors appear first, for fruit and vegetables.

Then molars come in, for grains—such as bread, rice, and pasta.

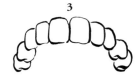

Finally all the teeth are in, at which point most children are ready to stop breastfeeding.

THE TONGUE

Most of the human body is covered with tough skin that does not change much from day to day. However, the mucous membranes and the skin right around them are highly sensitive and capable of rapid change. Any change in our health, especially one that affects mucus production in our bodies, affects the skin around the mucous membranes, making it crack or discharge mucus.

People don't like having others look at their genitals or anus but will usually allow you to examine another of their mucous membranes, which is the tongue. The tongue reveals much about the present condition of our health.

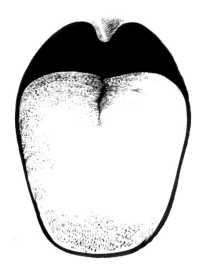

Tongue diagnosis: when stuck out, the tongue should not tremble or shake, and should be clear, with no coating.

Tongue zone diagnosis. The micro represents the macro. Project the entire body onto the tongue.

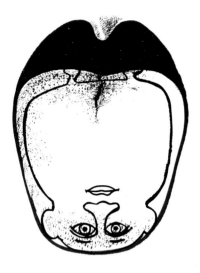

The tongue's dexterity is directly related to the condition of the heart. A strong heart reveals itself in good enunciation, but slurred speech often indicates some type of cardiovascular problem, including a murmur, irregular beating, angina, or inadequate blood supply, called coronary insufficiency. Sudden stuttering, too, reveals a weak heart caused by the consumption of too much liquid.

In my classes, I like to draw a tongue and then superimpose a human head over it, with the top of the head at the tip of the tongue and the mouth over the back of the tongue.

In Oriental diagnosis, we see the tip of the tongue as revealing the state of our current thinking. Often there are small red dots along the front edge of the tongue. These dots reveal a higher than average degree of stress, tension, and fear. We are thinking a lot; our brain and nervous system are taxed.

The middle area of the tongue corresponds to the digestive and respiratory systems. The back corresponds to the kidneys and reproductive system.

The tongue should be clean and clear. This indicates good digestion and circulation. It also reveals that the person is not eating too much.

Often, however, the tongue is coated or patched with a kind of white moss. Concentrations of moss in any of the above-mentioned areas reveal the corresponding part of the body as particularly stressed and stagnant.

There are two basic causes of white moss on the tongue:

1. Excessive amounts of fat, cholesterol, dairy products, and baked goods in the diet; these foods create congestion in the system. Fat and cholesterol from meat, eggs, and dairy foods block blood circulation and accumulate as plaque in capillaries, vessels, and arteries. Baked goods can be difficult to digest.

2. Overeating. The more you eat, the more difficult it is for your digestion to work properly. This is common sense. Wise men and women throughout history have always said that one of the secrets of longevity is a slightly empty stomach.

When there is a thick layer of white moss on the tongue, stagnation is especially acute in the digestive tract. The intestines are not able to fully eliminate; consequently, there is accumulation. The body attempts to eliminate the accumulation any way it can, including through the tongue. The same mechanism is at work when we have an upset stomach and suffer a bad taste in the mouth. The body is attempting to discharge the problem upward out of the mouth, causing the unpleasant taste.

Besides becoming covered with white moss, the tongue can turn other colors, including dark brown or black. Dark colors, especially black, indicate a serious discharge of toxins from the kidneys. Usually a blackened tongue suggests a serious problem. The kidney function is extremely weak and failing, and the person should seek immediate medical assistance.

The tongue can also turn yellow, indicating a problem with the liver, gallbladder, or spleen. The yellow tinge reveals excessive bile in the bloodstream.

From time to time you see canker sores developing on the tongue. Such skin eruptions indicate spleen and stomach problems, brought on by the consumption of too many acidic foods, such as spices, tomato sauce, eggplant, peppers, and sugar.

Once I was traveling in India and wanted to buy some souvenirs for my family and friends. I visited the local pharmacy and discovered a utensil designed to scrape the moss from the tongue. Indian people scrape the moss from their tongues so that they can eliminate accumulated waste and better appreciate the taste of their own cuisine! I was truly impressed. I bought many tongue scrapers that day and sent them to friends with the encouragment to scrape their tongues.

THE EARS

In Oriental diagnosis, a person's ears are among the most important and revealing aspects of the entire body. Every person's ears are unique. There are no two alike. Even your own two ears are slightly different from each other. The ears are bigger than fingerprints, and ears are always exposed. Many countries use the ear as an identifying aspect of the face in their passport photographs.

Just as the face is a paradox of diversity within similarity, so, too, are the ears, which have characteristics that can be read, just as the face can be read, to reveal the inner nature.

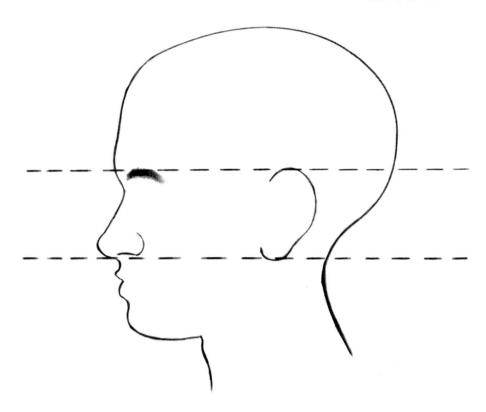

Ideally located ears.

Throughout Buddhist art, you will see the Buddha depicted with long and beautiful ears. His ears are round at the top, wide at the middle, and wonderfully tapered to the long lobes that dangle like heavy pendulums well down to his shoulders. These are the ears of an elephant on a human being! What does it mean? Why is the Buddha depicted with such enormous ears?

The answer is that in the Orient, including India, physiognomy or face reading, has always been understood and recognized as valid. The Buddha's face is the picture of bliss: his eyebrows are long and rounded, his eyes soft and gentle, his mouth narrow and closed. In terms of Oriental diagnosis, his face is the ultimate human face—reflecting the love, wisdom, peace, and fulfillment that are the eventual destiny of all humans traveling on the wheel of life. But then there are those ears, those long, strange ears. What are we to make of them? To the Oriental diagnostician, they are the confirmation of the inherited wealth of the Buddha's nature. The ears are meant to reveal the secret spiritual wealth with which the Buddha entered this life. Let me explain.

The ears have long been associated with the kidneys. Our two kidneys are in the mid-region of the back, just below the rib cage. Interestingly, the ears are about the same size and shape as the kidneys. In Japan, we say that to be a good listener, a person must have strong kidneys.

In Oriental medicine, the ears reveal the constitutional strength of the kidneys. The kidneys are the treasure chest of a person's ancestral inheritance. They distribute energy, or ki, throughout the body. In the same way, they parcel out the gifts of a person's ancestry in the form of talents and opportunities in life. A talent for music, art, teaching, building—whatever the ability is, it is here, housed in the kidneys and imbuing the person's life, thereby giving the life direction. We can say that a person's life path unfolds from his or her kidneys.

Long ears.

The ears also reveal the constitutional strength of the circulatory, digestive, and nervous systems. It is said in the Orient that the ear reveals the breadth of a person's understanding of people and life itself.

When we examine the ears, therefore, we are looking at much more than the outer horn of the hearing mechanism. We are looking at the strength of the kidneys and the ancestral inheritance of this particular person's life. It is a remarkable thing we are seeing, and we must look carefully if we want to truly understand this person.

In Oriental diagnosis, we say that the ear should be well shaped. It should be large. The top should be rounded, the middle fairly wide and tapering to the lobe. The earlobe should be ample. Let's look more carefully now at each of the ear's characteristics and its meaning.

To begin, let's use our guideline that the micro reveals the macro. When a baby is gestating, it is upside down in its mother's womb. The head is the most developed part of the body. The rest of the body is curved to present an image that looks very much like an ear, with the head represented by the earlobe and the circulatory and nervous systems represented by the two layers on the outer edge of the ear. The outermost section looks like a tire running along the outer edge of the ear; this overlapping rim represents the circulatory system.

When the rim is thick and wide, it reveals a strong, well-developed circulatory system. A person with a thick ear rim has a well-regulated body temperature. His or her extremities are warm and well nourished with blood. He or she has a strong, stable, and centered personality.

A good circulatory system generally means that a person mixes well with a wide variety of people. He or she understands others, is neither easily threatened nor threatening, and can make many friends in life.

Often you see a person with little or no rim at the edge of the ear. Occasionally you see a person with ears that point up and show no outer rim at all.

The absence of an outer rim indicates a weak circulatory system, caused by the mother's consumption of too many animal foods during pregnancy. Pointy ears, such as those of former national security adviser Zbigniew Brzezinski, are the result of an abundance of animal foods, especially beef and pork, consumed by the mother during pregnancy.

People with little or no circulatory rim tend to be cautious of others. Pointy-eared people can be highly suspicious of others, critical, and aggressive. They are often quick to argue or fight. They believe that

EAR ZONE DIAGNOSIS

the best defense is a good offense. They are constantly alert, ready to do battle. They can easily fall prey to paranoia. Their sharp intellects tend to see the darker elements in others but miss the brighter, more human side. These people must guard their health to safeguard their own sound judgment. They can too easily become one-sided in their outlook on life and fall victim to misanthropy.

At the top of the ear, just below the circulatory rim, is a horizontal ridge which continues downward along the edge of the ear toward the earlobe. The horizontal part of the ridge forms the upper third of the ear. It represents the nervous system. A well-developed ridge reveals a strong nervous system and a sharp mind. A person with such a ridge has a sound capacity to study and learn.

Sometimes the ridge in the upper ear has a raised wave within it, running up the middle of the ridge on an angle. This raised line looks like a minor mountain range within the exposed upper third of the ear. Such a line reveals a person with very pronounced intellectual abilities. This is a thinker, one who analyzes and gains insight into things. He or she does not take things at face value but explores their depths. However, such a person can be cold and overly critical. He or she needs to develop flexibility and tolerance.

Finally, in the center of the ear is another ridge line, this one running from the edge of the ear to the ear hole. If we use our micro-indicates-macro guideline, we find that this ridge on the fetus-shaped ear is right where the fetus's digestive system is. And this ridge indicates the strength of the digestive system.

In many people, this ridge is shallow and indistinct, indicating weak intestines. When the line is distinct and well developed, the intestines are natively strong, and the person possesses "guts," or courage. Such a person has the capacity to digest life—that is, to experience much of life and to understand it.

Next let's look at the overall size of the ear. The bigger, the better. A large ear indicates strong kidneys and a great understanding of life. This is especially true if both the ear and the earlobe are large. A person with an ample earlobe has a great deal of accumulated good fortune. He or she has a wide understanding of life. Such people also possess a marked degree of flexibility in their minds and actions. They tend to be involved in the "people" professions—the arts, law, philanthropy, public-related businesses, and the sciences that benefit people directly, such as medicine.

People with no earlobes, or "attached" lobes, have a narrower view of life. They tend to gravitate to the technical professions: accounting and computers, for example. If they are involved in science, they prefer solitary work in the laboratory, working on the more technical or arcane questions of science. Nevertheless, occasionally you see people with small earlobes in acting or writing or medicine. These people may be excellent at their work and possess much talent. But people with small earlobes tend to be singularly focused and have a driving ambition that excludes other aspects of their lives. Consequently, they have many emotional ups and downs. They experience many surprises in their relationships with others, largely because they do not understand other people as well as do those with larger ears and earlobes.

Ringing in the ears is a common problem today. The hidden cause can be in the kidneys.

Deep lines in front of the nub near the ear hole reveal disorders of the small intestines and heart. Lines or creases in the earlobe itself reveal a tendency toward diabetes.

Oriental diagnosis views the kidneys as the source of nourishment for the reproductive system. The kidneys provide ki to the sex organs, helping them maintain healthy function.

In the same way, the kidneys provide ki to nourish all the bones in the body. All bone disorders are seen as kidney-related problems. And since the ears are where one can "read" the kidneys, it is important to pay attention to the ears to understand their condition.

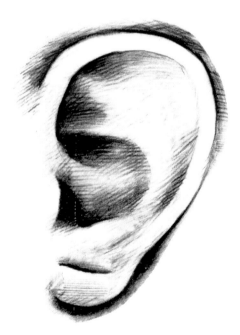

Horizontal line on the earlobe: diabetic problem.

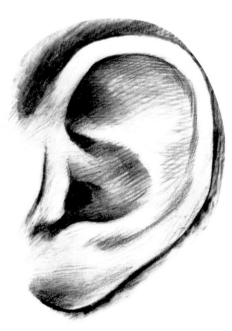

Vertical line in front of the nub near the ear hole: heart problem, high blood pressure.

EVOLUTION OF THE HUMAN FACE

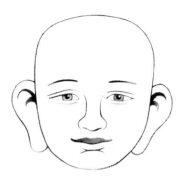

Our spiritual ancestors had beautiful, well-balanced, happy faces.

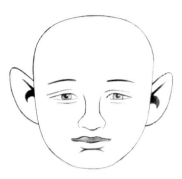

But nowadays we are deluged by information that comes to us from all over the world by telephone, satellite, computer, and fax machine. Trying to pay attention to all this makes us nervous, and our ears are becoming more and more pointed from the strain.

More meat consumption, more stress, more anger, and more aggression give us lines between the eyebrows, which are also becoming pointed due to our frustration. Oddly enough, some people pluck their eyebrows to make their faces even more ugly.

Increased consumption of meat and animal protein causes the canines to grow.

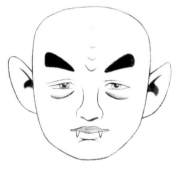

Bags develop under the eyes as a result of the nightlife life-style, overwork, fear, smoke, stress, and living out of harmony with the universe.

The use of drugs, alcohol, and sugar leads to an unbalanced life, and the eyes become sanpaku. What has become of the face of civilization? It is becoming a devil face! Let us think of the face of the future.

Meridian Diagnosis and the Five Transformations

EACH OF US HAS, AT ONE TIME OR ANOTHER, experienced a mysterious pain somewhere in our body for which we have no explanation. We haven't got the foggiest idea of how the pain originated, why it chose this particular place in the body, or how we can treat it, except by taking some type of painkiller. Other symptoms come and go without our understanding them, either. A rash, for example, may appear on the thumb, the leg, or the arm. Why in this place? you may ask. What caused the body to put that rash here? Do these things appear arbitrarily, or does the body have a reason for placing symptoms where it does?

When asking yourself such questions, it is good to keep in mind the fact that the human body is the most efficient and marvelous organism on the face of the earth. It doesn't do anything without cause. Our challenge is to understand the cause. All too often, we dismiss the actions of the body because we fail to understand how it works.

Oriental diagnosis is the practice of understanding how the body works at a very deep level. A rash on the hand or a mysterious pain behind the knee reveals a great deal about what is happening internally. Each says something about our behavior and our thinking. The key to interpreting these mysterious symptoms is learning how and where energy flows in the body. This is the understanding of meridian diagnosis, yet another key to reading the body.

ACUPUNCTURE MERIDIANS:
THE PATHWAYS OF KI

Let's consider, once again, heaven's and earth's force. The heavens are showering electromagnetic energy down on the earth in the form of solar rays and other planetary and stellar radiation. Meanwhile, the earth is surrounded by electromagnetic energy generated by the earth's north and south poles. In essence, our environment—the very air we breathe—is dynamically charged with energy: life force.

Each of us stands on the earth and acts as an antenna for the electromagnetic forces of heaven and earth, which charge our bodies from above and below. As I said in chapter 1, this electromagnetic energy that imbues our bodies is known in Japan as ki. In China it is called chi; in India, prana. This energy is essentially the life force that animates each of us.

Ki flows through our bodies in twelve distinct patterns, or meridians. Each meridian is like a river of energy that originates at a specific point in the body and flows downward or upward (depending on the meridian) to another point. These twelve rivers of ki bring life force to every cell in the body. When the river is blocked, the life force is prevented from getting to a specific area of the body. Cells, tissues, and whole organs suffocate from lack of ki. The result is some type of symptom.

In the early stges, the symptom is small—a rash perhaps, discomfort, or a nagging pain. Such minor symptoms are the body's way of telling us something isn't right. Life force sustains the immune system, so that bacteria or viruses that touch our skin are destroyed, as are pathogens we breathe into our systems. But when the life force is weak, immune cells are incapable of dealing with strong diseases and, consequently, pathogens have no trouble gaining a foothold in the body. The result is illness of one kind or another. Often the problem persists and even gets worse. Serious degeneration begins. Cells and tissues decay and eventually die, and the symptoms become much more serious: atrophy of muscles, heart disease, heart attack, stroke, diabetes, or cancer.

Again, think of a meridian as a river. When a river is dammed, water backs up so that one part of the river floods while another part goes dry. When a meridian is blocked, one part of the body is getting too much ki, while another part is getting too little. The resulting imbalance causes one organ to become overactive, while another can become lethargic or easily fatigued.

Often a person has a pain in a specific area of the body. He or she cannot determine why the pain is happening or why it is happening at that particular place. By knowing where the meridians flow, we can pinpoint which meridian or organ is affected and then decide how best to help such a person overcome the problem.

First we will look at the meridians as phenomena that relate to specific organs and functions. Further on in this chapter, we'll examine meridians in terms of their psychological and spiritual significance.

Below is a summary of the twelve meridians. Keep in mind that they are bilateral, meaning that there are two sets of identical meridians, one on each side of the body.

The lung meridian runs from a point on the breast just above the clavicle, along the inside of the arm to the thumb (see illustration). Symptoms—such as a discoloration, rash, infection, mole, or blemish—along this meridian suggest possible lung problems. (See specific exercises and dietary advice for the various meridians in chapter 9.)

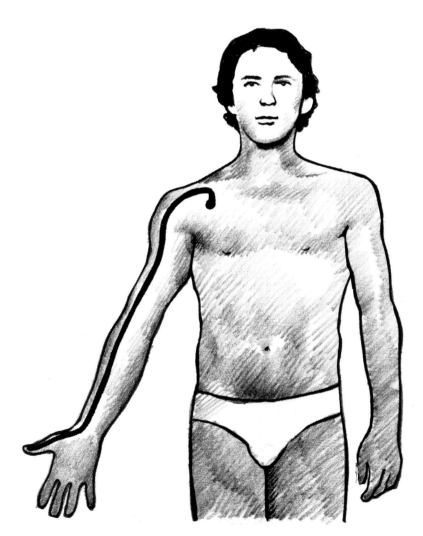

Lung meridian.

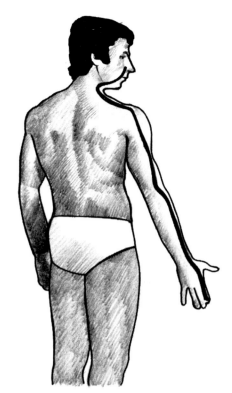

Large-intestine meridian.

The large-intestine meridian runs from the tip of the index finger along the outer part of the arm, then along the shoulder to the throat, neck, and outside of the mouth, and then to the crease at the nostril. Any symptom along this meridian can indicate a problem with elimination and breathing.

The kidney meridian runs from a point at the bottom of the foot, along the arch, to the heel, up the inside of the leg, to the sex organs, along the center of the stomach, to a point just below where the clavicle joins the sternum.

The kidneys cleanse the blood of impurities and help eliminate waste through the urine. As I mentioned in chapter 2, however, the role of the kidneys extends far beyond this important biological function. The kidneys extend ki throughout the body. They also provide spiritual direction in our lives by infusing our lives with the gifts of our ancestors—that is, our talents, opportunities, and challenges. Our life energy, or ki, comes from our kidneys. Consequently, the care of these vital organs is essential.

The spleen meridian runs from the outside of the big toe, up the inside of the foot, along the shinbone to the knee, up the inside of the thigh to the stomach area, and then runs on an angle to the outside of the armpit. Here it loops under the arm and runs down along the outside of the back. The spleen meridian is concerned with reproduction and digestion.

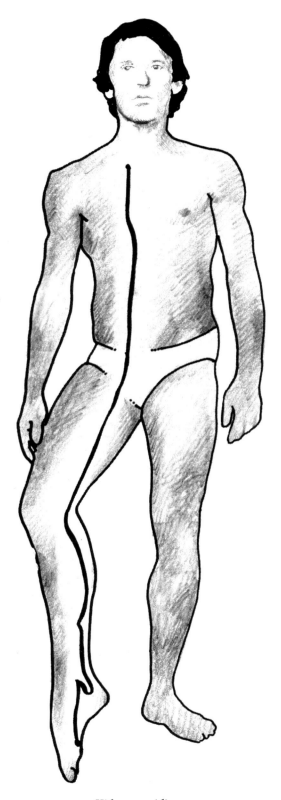

Kidney meridian.

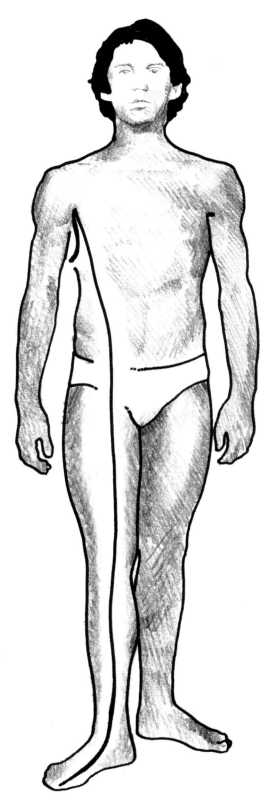

Spleen meridian.

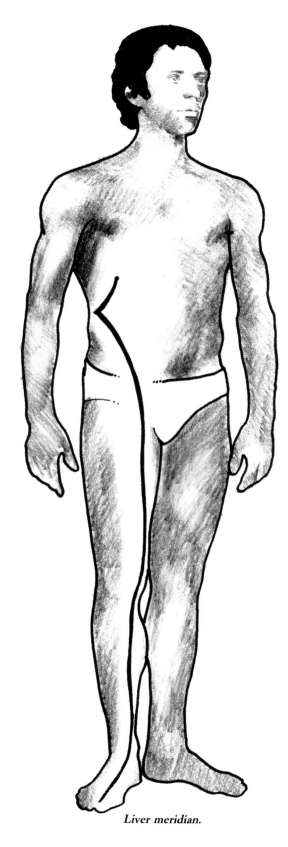

Liver meridian.

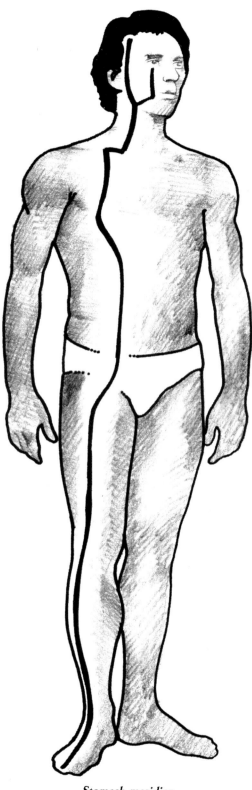

Stomach meridian.

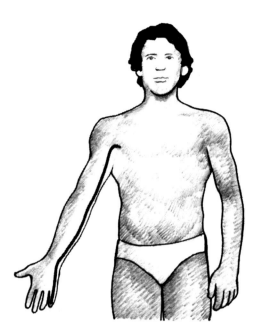

Heart meridian.

The liver meridian runs from the upper part of the big toe, up along the top of the foot, along the inner parts of the calf, thigh, and groin, to the outer part of the abdomen, to a point at the bottom of the rib cage (just below the liver), to a point between the sixth and seventh ribs, directly under the nipple. The liver meridian relates to the storage of nutrients and energy.

The stomach meridian forms a large U shape on each side of the face before it runs downward along the chest, thigh, and calf to a point at the top of the second toe. The inner channel of the U runs just below the eye to the tip of the outer corner of the mouth, and then to the chinbone. The outer channel of the U runs from the scalp down along the ear and face (where men wear sideburns) to the chin, where it joins the other channel. From here, the meridian runs along the neck to the clavicle and down directly across the nipple to the abdomen, across the groin, down along the thigh and calf, and on to the second toe. The stomach meridian is concerned with the appetite and the intake of food.

The heart meridian runs from the armpit, along the inside of the arm, to the inside of the wrist, to a point on the inside of the little finger just above the nail. This meridian provides ki to the heart and assists in circulation.

The small-intestine meridian runs from the upper part of the little finger, just above the nail, up the outside of the arm, along the tricep, to a point in the center of the shoulder blade on the back, up the neck, to a point directly in front of the ear hole. This meridian is concerned with the assimilation of nutrients.

The bladder meridian runs from the inside corner of the eye, up the forehead, over the top of the head and down the center of the back. Here it divides to form two parallel lines on the right side of the back and two more on the left side, so that, in all, it comprises four meridian lines. Each set of two runs along the back, down the buttocks, and down the back of each leg. Each set of two meridian lines joins at the back of the knee, becoming one meridian line on each leg. From the knee the bladder meridian runs along the calf, to the back of the ankle, along the outside of the foot, to the little toe. The bladder meridian is concerned with elimination.

The gallbladder meridian runs from the temple around the outside of the ear, down the back of the head, then back up the side of the head, stopping just above the temple and then running back down to the neck. This up-and-down motion along the side of the head creates a thin crescent-moon shape (see illustration). From here, the meridian runs over the front of the shoulder, down the side of the abdomen in a zigzag motion, to the hip, and then down the outside of the leg, to the fourth toe. This meridian is concerned with the distribution of energy.

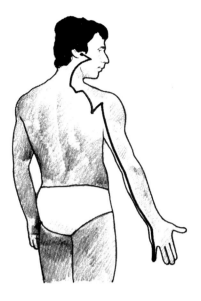

Small-intestine meridian.

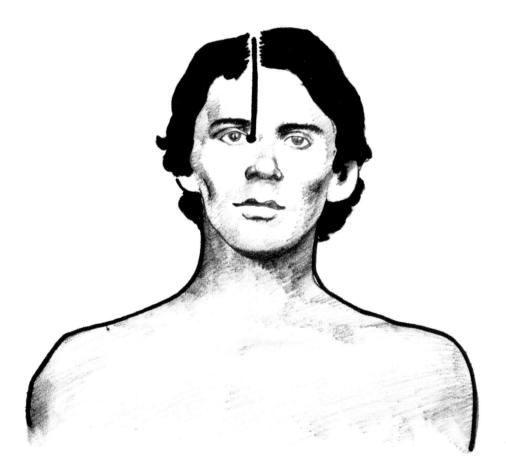

Bladder meridian.

• • •

Besides these ten, there are two more meridians whose primary purpose is to unify systems and functions within the body.

The heart constrictor meridian runs from the armpit, down the middle of the inside of the arm, across the middle of the palm, to the tip of the middle finger. The heart constrictor meridian assists the heartbeat, circulation, and assimilation of nutrition. It also provides ki, assists in blood flow to the pericardium, and helps the heart function.

The triple heater meridian runs from the top of the fourth finger up the arm to the shoulder, up the neck, and around the top of the ear to the temple. The triple heater meridian provides ki to the small-intestine meridian and the lymphatic system, and assists circulation to the extremities. The triple heater also coordinates the three heating systems, which maintain the body temperature. One is above the solar plexus, the second is in between the solar plexus and the navel, and the third is below the navel.

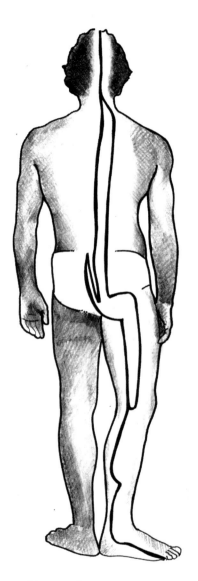

Bladder meridian.

Once you understand the meridians, you can learn why the body manifests a symptom in a specific place and how best to heal it.

The whole understanding of meridian diagnosis is meant to demonstrate that we humans are intimately connected with the universe as a whole. We are one with it. The universe is filled with an invisible energy, ki, that binds all phenomena. At the same time, everything is evolving according to an orderly scheme which is governed by this great spirit, the universe. The universe is a unity, an integrated body, with which we are joined. In traditional and spiritual cultures, people have always maintained that humans have the unique capacity to perceive and experience oneness with this whole. We call this enlightenment. Enlightenment is that stage of consciousness in which we recognize that we are no longer separate from anything within the universe—that is, each of us realizes that he or she is the universe.

Even without being truly enlightened, we can use this consciousness—that is, our unity with the universe—to heal ourselves, and to find answers to our most fundamental questions. In Oriental diagnosis, we examine the body from this enlightened perspective. There is nothing random about a line on the face, or a pain in the left hand. It is a symptom that relates to the whole body, and to a specific part.

Energy doesn't merely pour down from heaven or ascend from the earth in torrents through the body, but is channeled in an orderly fashion by this incredible machine. There is a pattern by which the body channels energy throughout its every fiber. That orderly pattern is known as the Five Elements or Five Transformations.

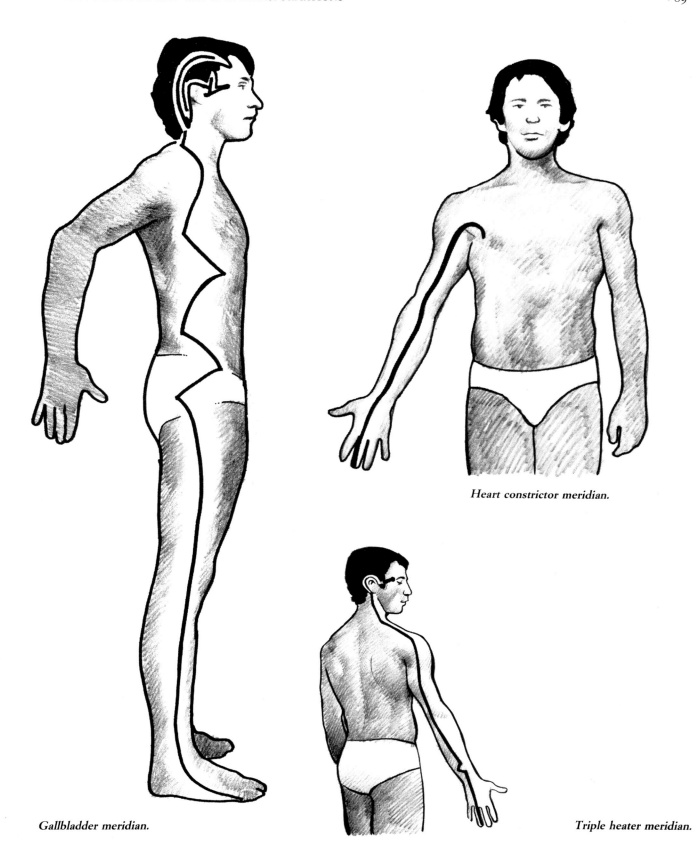

Gallbladder meridian.

Heart constrictor meridian.

Triple heater meridian.

THE FIVE ELEMENTS, OR FIVE TRANSFORMATIONS

More than two thousand years ago, Chinese sages formulated a theory that sought to explain the stages of change. These ancient philosophers began with the premise that change occurred in an orderly and predictable manner. They looked at nature and saw that the seasons progressed in an orderly cycle; that the growth and development of human beings also took place in an organic and orderly pattern—that is, from infancy to puberty, to adolescence, adulthood, and old age.

Personal psychology also seemed to follow consistent patterns. An idea evolved through certain clear stages on the way to becoming a reality. Change is not a random thing, said the ancient sages, but an orderly process—an evolution. The Chinese formulated a theory of change and called it Five Elements, or Five Transformations.

Like much of traditional Oriental thought, the Five Transformations reflected the Chinese ability to classify phenomena and at the same time remain flexible. The theory has been used in healing, personal psychology, agriculture, economics, and politics. It has been employed to treat disease, predict the weather, and divine personal fortune. In short, it is a cosmology, an attempt to understand life and the universe.

At its most abstract, the Five Transformations theory posits that all change occurs in five stages. Each stage is associated with a particular element in nature—fire, earth, metal, water, or wood.

The process begins with the original inspiration, the world of ideas. At this stage, the thing in question is still amorphous, plasmic, and yet possessed of great energy to inspire action. The sages looked for an analogy in nature and found fire, which, though highly amorphous, is nevertheless possessed of great energy that inspires change. From fire, the cycle moves on to a more solid, grounded state, in which the idea begins to take shape as a perceivable reality. This stage is known as earth. From earth, the process continues to its most dense and material form, signified as metal. The metallic state suggests the greatest condensation, or "yangization," of the process, in which the idea firmly takes root in the material world. The thing in question is born. It is real.

From the metal phase, the process continues to water, its most flexible and enduring stage. Water signifies the continuity of change toward a specific goal, for water is always flowing toward the ocean. From water, the evolutionary process moves on to the wood phase, in which we see the fruits of the dream. Here, the original inspiration has gone through its necessary development to bring forth rewards. Wood signifies the culmination of the cycle, for wood not only bears fruit but fertilizes the soil with its leaves, seeds, and unused fruit, to enrich the soil and begin the process of regeneration all over again.

If we were to apply the Five Transformations theory to a business, a shoe store for example, we would say that the fire stage is the moment when the seminal idea takes hold in the mind of the prospective store owner. This is the point of original inspiration, the moment of great excitement that comes with the birth of a new idea. The earth phase marks the stage in which the owner actually plans his or her business and arranges the financing. He or she has now brought the idea from the abstract to the practical or earthly realm. The metal stage marks the opening of the doors to the public. Now the idea is real in all its dimensions. The person is finally selling shoes. The water stage signifies the daily process of doing business, of staying in business and dealing with the public—a feat that requires great flexibility (the flexibility of water), endurance, and ingenuity. The shoe-store owner must now persist in time while keeping his or her sights set on the original goal, namely the success of the business.

The wood phase brings that success, the stage at which the enterprise bears fruit. The shoe store is not only in the black, but is generating more than enough money to provide for its owner, its employees and the community at large. From wood the cycle continues to fire—the birth of a new idea, and with it a new cycle of change.

While the Five Elements, or Five Transformations, traditionally have wide application, I will confine my discussion to health and personality development.

In terms of health, the Five Transformations reveal how energy moves through the body, nourishing each organ system in an orderly and methodical fashion. For the body can be understood as an integrated circuitry system, in which ki, or life force, flows through the system continuously according to an orderly pattern. Health is the state in which ki flows unimpeded through the system and thus fully nourishes every organ and cell in the body.

The schema is the same: fire, earth, metal, water, and wood. In terms of physical health, each element is associated with a group of organs, which, in their turn, nourish each other and form an integrated whole. The five stages and their related organ systems are as follows:

Fire: The heart, circulatory system, and small intestine. The heart and small intestine are joined and are regarded as related organ systems in Oriental medicine. They are seen as nourishing each other. The heart is the yang, or contracted organ, while the small intestine is the yin, or expanded organ. While they nourish each other, they also pass energy on to the earth stage. For this reason, we say that the fire organs are the mother of the earth organs, because they provide life force to the earth organs.

Earth: The stomach, spleen, and pancreas. The earth organs are the mother of the metal organs.

Metal: The lungs and large intestine. The metal organs are the mother of the water organs.

Water: The kidneys and bladder. The water organs are the mother of the wood organs.

Wood: The liver and gallbladder. The wood organs are mother of the fire organs, or heart, circulatory system, and small intestine. With this, the cycle completes itself and continues.

If every element is working optimally, no symptoms occur and there is optimal health. If, on the other hand, one or more of the stages is blocking energy, the corresponding organ system will suffer. Consequently, those who damage their liver often suffer from heart and small intestine troubles, while those who damage their spleen, stomach, and pancreas also suffer from diseases of the large intestine and lungs.

Looking at the body according to the Five Transformations, we can easily see the harmony within the human systems and come to know the importance of each organ to the body as a whole.

For example, typically we should say that digestion is performed by the stomach and intestines, but according to the Five Transformations, digestion absolutely depends on the healthy functioning of the spleen.

Biologically, we know that the spleen filters damaged and dead cells out of the blood and infuses the blood with immune cells, such as lymphocytes and other white cells. In Western medicine, the spleen is not considered essential to life and is often surgically removed, as in the case of certain cancers and other disorders.

However, Oriental medicine regards the spleen as one of the supremely important organs and essential to the orderly functioning of life. Spleen energy—that is, ki emanating from the spleen—governs the movement of food through digestion. The spleen energy helps to transport the food through the intestinal tract. As it does this, it also assists the small intestine in turning the essence of food—that is, the essential nutrients—into blood and ki. The spleen sends ki to the lungs and large intestine. In this way, it nourishes these two organs with life force, making possible both breathing and elimination of waste.

Energy must move freely from the spleen to adequately nourish the lungs and large intestine. This spleen energy is needed to create peristalsis and move waste through the bowel and out of the body.

You may say to yourself, "I thought the intestine did that on its own." If you looked strictly at the large intestine, you'd be right. But the degree to which the large intestine is able to perform peristalsis depends on the energy it receives from the spleen.

Usually, if the spleen is troubled, there will be excessive gas, acidic stomach, or some other digestive problem, such as heartburn.

If digestion is troubled, therefore, we must treat both the intestinal tract and the earth element. Spleen energy requires an alkaline condition in the body. The more acidic the blood, the more the spleen suffers. Therefore, chewing food well is essential to the health of the spleen, since saliva is an alkaline substance. The less chewing, the less saliva, and the poorer the health of the spleen. (See chapter 9 for dietary suggestions for health and for exercises that treat specific meridians and organ systems.)

In Oriental medicine, spleen energy also governs the blood. When there is hemorrhaging, uterine bleeding, or another bleeding problem, Oriental medicine recommends treating the spleen, for the spleen contains and channels the blood through the body. If the spleen energy is weak, blood will break free from its capillaries, causing bleeding from some soft part of the body.

If the spleen, stomach, and pancreas are excessively stimulated over time, they will eventually become so weak that they will be unable to pass energy on to the lungs and large intestines, causing these organs to suffer in turn.

The relationship between the spleen and large intestine is essentially the same one that exists between the large intestine and kidneys; the kidneys and liver; the liver and heart; and the heart and spleen. Each one nourishes the other with ki, making optimal functioning possible.

In this nourishing cycle, energy moves clockwise from the fire element to earth to metal to water to wood and back to fire. The nourishing cycle provides optimal amounts of life force so that each organ group flourishes. But there is another, complementary cycle, called the *Ko,* or controlling cycle, in which organ systems are restricted or held in check. In this way, each organ group is kept in balance with the others within the system. In the controlling cycle, energy moves within the interior of the Five Elements, or Five Transformations, circle and serves to keep each organ system within prescribed limits. We can easily see a corollary for this in nature.

The water that flows in a river has power because of two factors: the quantity of water that nourishes the river (this corresponds with the nourishing cycle of the Five Elements, or Five Transformations); and the presence of strong banks, which provide limits to the water and thus give it direction, power, and speed. If the banks give way, or if the river crests its banks, the water no longer has the same power or orderliness. It simply floods an area and sits, until it eventually recedes. Movement sharply declines and then stops, until evaporation or gravity causes the water to go in other directions.

As long as limits are imposed on the water, it has tremendous power to move obstacles or to drive hydroelectric pumps to generate electricity. The "Ko," or controlling cycle, works in the same way. The controlling cycle balances the system by maintaining limits on the energy that flows to organ systems. While energy flows clockwise within the nourishing cycle, the controlling cycle causes energy to move within the circle of the Five Elements, or Five Transformations.

Specifically, ki, or life force, within the controlling cycle moves in the following manner:

Fire controls metal: The heart and small intestine function controls or limits energy within the lungs and large intestine.

Soil controls water: The stomach, spleen, and pancreas function limits or controls the energy implicit in the kidneys and bladder.

Metal controls wood: The lung and large intestine function controls or limits the energy flowing in the liver and gallbladder.

Water controls fire: The kidney and bladder function controls the energy implicit in the heart and small intestine.

Wood controls earth: The liver and gallbladder function controls the energy flowing in the stomach, spleen, and pancreas.

For the purposes of healing, the controlling cycle is essential. Let's look at an example. In the case of diarrhea, the metal element (lungs and large intestine) may be hyperactive. This is often caused by excessive energy in the spleen, which passes that excess on to the large intestine, causing it to function hyperactively. Spleen imbalance can be caused by the intake of too many sweets, or too much fruit juice or alcohol or some other yin substance that excites the spleen, causing it to overwork and stimulate the large intestine excessively. When the metal element is hyperactive, it controls or diminishes energy flowing to the wood element, or the liver and gallbladder. Thus, the liver function is diminished. The heart and small intestine (or fire element) is weakened as well, because the fire element is nourished by the liver and gallbladder, which now are unable to pass much energy along to the heart and small intestine functions. This will cause a variety of digestive problems and weak nutrient assimilation. The real problem is in the spleen, which must be treated by eliminating sweet foods and drinks, and increasing the consumption of alkalizing foods (miso soup, tamari broth, whole grains chewed well, and a variety of vegetables). (See chapter 9 for dietary guidelines.)

Another clear example of how the controlling cycle affects another organ system is the relationship between the water and fire elements.

Often people eat too much salt, which causes kidney disorders. The kidney and bladder function (the water element) controls the heart and small intestine function (the fire element). Consequently, kidney disorders, especially those arising from excess salt intake, causes illnesses of the fire element, such as heart disease and high blood pressure. If we wish to treat this condition, we must treat the controlling element, which in this case is the water element. By sharply reducing the consumption of salt, oils, and fats and by increasing mild aerobic exercise (the fire element), we strengthen both the water and fire elements and their corresponding organ systems.

To practice Oriental diagnosis, we must be aware of the awesome integration that exists within the human body. We must be aware of the immediate physical problems and their causes, but also of the underlying relationships involved in the cause of the problem. The Five Elements, or Five Transformations, provides the keys to this deeper understanding. For this reason, the Five Elements, or Five Transformations, formed the foundation of Oriental medicine and many of its philosophical tenets. It is the basis for understanding human health and, indeed, natural change.

KI ENERGY, PERSONAL PSYCHOLOGY, AND SPIRIT

As I mentioned, the Five Transformations is a very flexible tool with an incredibly wide application. Let's look at how it can be applied to personal psychology.

In addition to the groupings of organs I have just discussed, each element is also associated with a specific emotional state. The emotions associated with each element are as follows:

Fire: Joy and hysteria. The heart and small intestine are the sources within the body of joy. When the heart is balanced and functioning well, it is easier for us to experience joy in our lives. When the heart and small intestine are functioning poorly, we find it difficult—sometimes impossible—to find joy in our lives. When Oriental healers found a person suffering from chronic unhappiness, they recognized that there was nothing in that person's life that inspired him or her, nothing that provided a new direction. There was no fire in the person's life. Therefore, the healers treated the heart, or fire element.

Occasionally the fire element can become overstimulated. In this case, we experience hysteria—wild displays of emotion, totally out of control. Again, this indicates a serious imbalance in the fire element, which must be considered if the condition is to be healed.

Earth: Thinking and sympathy, understanding, and romantic compassion. When the spleen is overstimulated (often from excess sugar and sweet foods), the person is often sentimental and excessively sympathetic, to the point that he or she weakens others. When the spleen is strong, there is a deep understanding and compassion for others, but not a syrupy sentimentality. This person knows when another person needs loving support, and when he or she needs some discipline.

Metal: Grief. Everyone suffers some sadness in life. It is a necessary part of being human, it seems. But it is important to keep our sadness and grief in perspective and to let go of our pain if we are to live productive lives. If a person clings to his or her grief, the large intestine is usually troubled. By improving the health of this organ, we improve our ability to let go of unnecessary emotions and to get on with our lives. Therefore, when treating grief, treat the large intestine and encourage the person to let go of lingering pain.

Water: Surprise and fear. It has been known for decades that stress and fear are destructive to the kidneys and adrenal glands. Chronic stress or fear can cause kidney damage. When the kidneys are weak, we experience more fear, are easily surprised, have less determination, and experience loss of will. The kidneys, as the seat of the will, help direct us through life, especially when we face adversity. Therefore, in times of difficulty and stress, protect the kidneys. If a person suffers chronic fear, I recommend treating the kidneys.

Wood: Anger. When the liver and gallbladder are troubled or damaged, there is an increase in anger and hostility. And anger itself can injure the liver and gallbladder. Alcohol, for example, injures the liver and, if consumed in excess, results in sudden outbreaks of anger. One must only spend a few days with an alcoholic to know that the dominant emotions are anger, bitterness, and rage. Those who suffer from chronic anger must treat their livers.

Since the organ systems also relate to their respective meridians, we can easily join the Five Transformations to meridian diagnosis to gain a truly holistic understanding of mind and body.

Up until now, I have discussed acupuncture meridians from the standpoint of physical health. But there is another way of looking at meridians and organs that is more abstract and spiritual and just as valid and revealing. To understand this way of diagnosis, you must see that each of your organs has both a physical and an abstract function. When I say abstract here, I mean spiritual.

Let me give you a general example. The role of your digestive system is to take food from your environment, digest it, make the nutrients available to your blood, and eliminate what is unnecessary. That is a very spiritual task! It signifies, in essence, your capacity to get what you need for your life, make it available to yourself for your own survival and happiness, and eliminate what you do not need. It plays an essential role in your physical, psychological, and spiritual well-being. "How effective am I at getting what I need in life?" you might ask yourself. "How effective am I at eliminating what I do not need, such as those experiences and habits that no longer serve my stage of development?" When you've answered this question, ask yourself how strong your digestion is.

Your digestive system is only a physical metaphor for a spiritual function. All your organs can be looked at from this perspective. Each organ and bodily function that makes up your body is only a physical manifestation of a spiritual quality that was inherent in your soul when you joined the earth at your conception.

Let's take the kidneys as another example. One of the major functions of the kidneys is to filter impurities from the blood. The kidneys are essential to life. In a more abstract way, we can say that the kidneys' function is to cleanse our blood by recognizing what is good and what is unnecessary or even harmful. If the kidneys are not working well, we have a hard time differentiating between the good and the bad in our lives. In other words, our judgment is affected by our poorly functioning kidneys. Old impurities in our personalities and our environment—even toxic elements—remain with us. We are at a loss to recognize or eliminate them. Consequently, we are constantly being surprised, sometimes even shocked, by unforeseen dilemmas. This causes fear and, in the extreme, paranoia. We feel like victims of life; actually, we are victims of our own poor judgment.

To illustrate these points for my students, I often place a sheet over my body and then perform certain mime exercises that the students recognize as common functions in their lives. The sheet covers the details of my body and reveals the essential motions associated with common functions. For example, with the sheet over me, I mime the functions of grasping for food and eating. This is the function of taking nourishment. Or I mime the function of sitting on the toilet. This is the function of eliminating what I do not need. The students get a big laugh out of this, but they realize, too, that when I am trying to grasp for something, the front of my body is the most active. When I am trying to eliminate, the emphasis is on my back and backside. Thus, the stomach meridian—the meridian that serves to bring food to us— is in the front, while the bladder meridian—the meridian that helps eliminate waste from our bodies—runs along the back.

I am teaching them that meridians are not merely channels of energy, but phenomena unto themselves. Meridians are the places where energy gathers to make the body function appropriately. Once the function is complete, the meridian line ceases to be as active.

As we have seen before, each organ and meridian can have too much energy—what is called *jitsu* in Japanese—or too little, called *kyo*. When an organ has too much energy, the activity associated with that organ or meridian is excessive, too. The organ may be overworked or energy may be trapped there, causing a blockage and thus preventing other organs from being adequately nourished with life force. The organ becomes overworked. In the same way, the psychological aspect of that organ is also overemphasized.

If the organ is kyo, or depleted, the organ is weak, lethargic, and likely stagnant with blood. The psychological aspect is that we may be weak in the area of life associated with this organ or meridian.

If I know the physical symptoms associated with a depleted stomach, for example, I can ask my friend if he or she also suffers from the psychological conditions associated with this organ. I can then advise him or her to enhance the condition of the specific organ—the stomach, for example—which in turn will enhance psychological well-being.

By seeing organs and meridians in their abstract nature, I can tell much about a person's psychological and spiritual well-being.

Let's look at the individual meridians in terms of their psychological and spiritual meanings.

(For remedies for each of the problems outlined below, see chapter 9.)

THE LUNG MERIDIAN

The lungs clean the blood by infusing it with oxygen and removing carbon dioxide. In Oriental medicine, we say that the inhalation of oxygen is the taking in of ki, or life force. If you hold your breath, you get a very quick demonstration of how dependent you are on oxygen and on your lungs. If we look at this in an abstract, or spiritual, way, we can say that the lungs take in life. When the lungs are not working properly, therefore, our ability to take in life is diminished. This has widespread physical and psychological effects.

When the Lung Energy Is Depleted, or Kyo

People with depleted lung energy have difficulty eliminating carbon dioxide. Consequently, the blood is poorly oxygenated and carbon dioxide remains in the blood to form a fertile breeding ground for colds, viruses, and microorganisms. As a result, people with lung problems are highly susceptible to colds.

Breathing also eliminates tension. When breathing is difficult, tension builds, especially in the shoulders.

When lung energy is depleted, people tend to be overweight. They sense a heaviness in their heads, due to poor circulation and lack of oxygen. They suffer from lung congestion and coughing. When the lung is depleted, congestion is chronic. There isn't sufficient energy in the lung to eliminate the underlying stagnation. The cough is hard and doesn't bring up much mucus.

The psychological symptoms associated with depleted lung energy are anxiety, loss of mental acuity, depression, and hypersensitivity. Shortness of breath tends to cause emotional imbalances, even hysteria.

When the Lungs Are Excessive in Energy, or Jitsu

Hard coughing that brings up mucus is generally a sign of excess energy trapped in the lungs. Often a hard smoker's cough—especially if the person is strong and otherwise healthy—comes from excess energy in the lung. A person with such a cough suffers from nasal congestion, too. He or she is prone to bronchitis and asthma. The chest muscles are often tight, especially around the lung meridian.

People with excessive lung energy can become obsessive and anxious over details. They have trouble releasing pent-up energy. They sigh a lot, often in an effort to let go of the tension in the lungs. They feel oppressed and have trouble expressing their love physically. They also are a bit apprehensive.

THE LARGE-INTESTINE MERIDIAN

The principal functions of the large intestine are eliminating waste and absorbing water and some nutrients. (The small intestine is the principal organ of absorption.) As I mentioned earlier in my discussion of the Five Elements, or Five Transformations, the large intestine has a complementary relationship with the lungs. Problems with the large intestine often affect the lungs and sinuses.

The large intestine and the lungs are the organs associated with the emotions of grief. If the large intestine and lung function is not healthy, there is a tendency to hold on to grief, sadness, and the experiences related to such emotions.

When the Large-Intestine Energy Is Depleted, or Kyo

When the large intestine is depleted of energy, we generally experience constipation; dry, congested nasal passages; and bronchial congestion. People with weak large intestines often suffer from diarrhea when they eat fibrous or coarse foods. Those with weak large intestines suffer from coolness in the area of the abdomen.

All over the world, people associate courage with having "guts." Having guts means having the determination and will to go through difficulties and prevail. A weak large intestine causes people to lose determination and courage. They often feel disappointed and dependent, and eventually may succumb to despair and bitterness.

When the Large Intestine Is Excessive in Energy, or Jitsu

Too much energy in the large intestine causes headaches, runny nose, nasal congestion, nosebleeds, tonsillitis, gum and tooth pain, whitish eyes and complexion, shoulder pain, stiffness in the chest, constipation that shifts to diarrhea, coughing, hemorrhoids, and the symptoms of the common cold. Problems in the large intestine directly affect the functioning of the lungs, bronchi and nasal passages. The reason:

trapped, excessive energy in the large intestine travels upward when it cannot be eliminated downward. The body tries to remedy the situation and restore balance by bringing the energy to the upper organs—hence the symptoms in the lungs, throat, and nose.

The psychological problem associated with excessive energy in the large intestine is continual dissatisfaction. The person cannot appreciate anything—himself or herself, work, parents, or friends. Eventually, unable to appreciate anyone's good points, especially his or her own, the person becomes isolated and friendless.

The reason is simple: the large intestine spends too much time and energy working on the waste of the body. When its energy is excessive, it cannot let go. It becomes obsessive in its job of sorting through what is essentially waste—the feces. The psychological effect on the person is that he or she dedicates too much energy to pettiness, resentment, and negative or useless memories. The person devotes too much attention and energy to that which should be overlooked or forgotten.

THE KIDNEY MERIDIAN

As I mentioned earlier, the kidneys purify the blood. So do the adrenal glands on the kidneys, which manufacture adrenaline, the hormone responsible for instantaneous reaction in a crisis.

In Oriental medicine, we say that the kidneys control fear and courage. They also house the spiritual gifts and karma accumulated from previous incarnations and handed down from the ancestors. Therefore, the kidneys are regarded as among the most important of all the organs.

When the Kidney Energy Is Depleted, or Kyo

The skin of those with weak kidney energy is often brown and lacks elasticity. Such people have poor circulation, especially in the hips and hara; frequent urination; and lower-back ache. The kidneys govern the sex organs and thus influence hormonal balance. When kidney energy is depleted, sex drive is also weak. People with weak kidney energy have trouble getting a deep sleep. The kidneys also influence the health of the bones. Weak kidneys lead to bone diseases, including osteoporosis and fractures. People with weak kidney energy are often prone to accidents.

Kidneys also govern the organs associated with hearing. When kidney energy is weak, there can be poor circulation in the ears, a loss of hearing at the higher frequencies, and sometimes ringing in the ears.

Psychologically, those with weak kidney energy are chronically anxious and fearful. They also suffer from a lack of determination. They usually have family troubles because they lack patience and endurance.

When the Kidney Energy Is Excessive, or Jitsu

Those with excessive kidney energy often experience chronic thirst, chronic ringing in the ears, poor hearing, tightness in the lower back and torso, dark urine, a bitter taste in the mouth, bad breath, and chronic fatigue from overwork. They often have a dark color to their skin, especially beneath the eyes.

Psychologically, such people tend to be workaholics. They are nervous, driven, and perfectionistic. They are moved by fear of failure or by a sense that some disaster is about to befall them.

THE SPLEEN MERIDIAN

The spleen cleans the blood of damaged or destroyed cells. It mediates the infusion of immune cells into the bloodstream. It is essential to proper digestion, especially because it nourishes both the stomach and large intestine with life force, or ki. Women with weak spleen meridian activity tend to suffer from menstrual problems. Men with weak spleen meridian activity tend to suffer from impotence.

I maintain that the emotions associated with the spleen are compassion and sympathy. People with weak spleens tend to be overly sympathetic. Those with balanced spleen conditions have a strong compassion for others but seek to understand the meaning of life's underlying difficulties.

When the Spleen Energy Is Depleted, or Kyo

When a person's spleen energy is weak, he or she suffers poor digestion, lack of saliva, poor ability to taste food, chronic acid stomach, brownish color in the face, great susceptibility to colds, a stiff and sensitive navel, pain in the spine, and poor circulation in the feet.

Psychologically, the person may be obsessed with details, chronically anxious, and restless; may think too much; may spend sleepless nights, causing chronic fatigue; and may suffer from cold limbs and poor circulation. He or she may be overly sympathetic and weak, and may indulge too much in gossip, all the while justifying the indulgence by saying that he or she is really offering a sympathetic ear.

When the Spleen Energy Is Excessive, or Jitsu

When the spleen has an excess of energy, greater than normal amounts of saliva fill the mouth, as the spleen tries to restore balance to its condition. The stomach tends to be acidic, sensitive, and nervous. There is a heaviness in the legs, and a chronic craving for sweets. The person probably suffers from hypoglycemia from eating too many sweets. Consequently, he or she may be moody and subject to great swings in energy level. Again, the person may indulge too much in sympathy—

for self or for others—and have the attitude that effort and understanding are futile.

THE LIVER MERIDIAN

The liver is truly a master organ. It performs so many intricate and amazing duties, including storing energy, cleansing the blood, and creating immune cells and digestive enzymes.

In the Orient, we say that the liver is the seat of the soul. The emotion associated with the liver and gallbladder is anger. Too much anger injures the liver. Conversely, equanimity causes the liver to relax and function better.

When the Liver Energy Is Depleted, or Kyo

When a person's liver energy is weak, he or she is easily fatigued, because the liver is not releasing glycogen, or stored fuel. Such people also suffer from dizziness, tired eyes, and a tendency to have accidents. The body is easily poisoned because the liver is unable to detoxify the blood. Hepatitis and other serious liver diseases are more easily contracted and difficult to get rid of. People with weak liver energy contract fevers, and have weak sexual vitality, impotence, and prostate trouble.

Psychologically, a person with a weak liver becomes irritable and angry very easily. Such people are given to inconsistency and nervousness. They are unable to gain weight. They devote far too much attention to trivial details.

When the Liver Energy is Excessive, or Jitsu

When the liver energy is excessive, a person is driven, obsessive, and a workaholic. He or she is given to excessive drinking, especially of alcohol. Such people likely suffer from heaviness in the head, poor digestion, and occasional bouts of dizziness. Since the meridian energy is excessive, there is a pulling throughout the meridian, causing a tightness in the anus, hemorrhoids, and, in men, prostate problems and discomfort in the testicles. Women with excessive liver energy have ovarian problems, sometimes cysts, inflammation in the reproduction organs, and premenstrual syndrome. Both men and women have a tightness in hara, flatulence, and putrefaction of tissues, causing body odor.

Psychologically, such people are stubborn, aggressive, prone to anger, highly emotional in general, and, ironically, hypersensitive. They are good eaters with enormous appetites. They make constant efforts to control anger and emotional outbursts. This repression eventually gives way to explosions of anger, after which these people are apologetic and remorseful.

THE STOMACH MERIDIAN

The stomach's role, of course, is to receive partially digested food (that is, chewed food) and prepare it for the small intestine. The stomach secretes acid that breaks down the food and makes it more accessible to the bloodstream once it arrives in the small intestine.

The stomach is one of those organs that we cannot ignore. Any stomach problem tends to disturb us, and chronic stomach ills disturb us throughout the day.

When the Stomach Energy Is Depleted, or Kyo

When a person's stomach is depleted of energy, the person has little appetite, is finicky about what he or she eats, and usually suffers chronic discomfort from gastric acid secretion. The legs are often heavy, and the body fatigues easily. The person often has stomach pain, and, if he or she eats the wrong foods, can suffer acutely for hours. Usually stomach problems are associated with related digestive problems— constipation, diarrhea, or spastic colon.

Stomach problems have very direct effects on our psyches. People with depleted stomach energy are moody, cranky, and tend to think too much, especially about themselves. Because they tire easily, they suffer from the perception that they are weak. They often lack confidence. They crave soft and cold foods, such as ice cream and soft drinks, but overall they have poor appetites. They need rest and prefer to recline when sitting, even when they are in a straight-backed chair.

These people have trouble receiving what they need. The stomach function is weak, causing them to feel undernourished and poorly cared for by life. They are often frustrated. They do not enjoy the struggles of life, but instead see everything as an inconvenience.

When the Stomach Energy Is Excessive, or Jitsu

Excess stomach energy causes an emphasis on the stomach. The person with too much stomach energy tends to overeat, though again there may be little appetite. The person may have stiffness in the shoulders and some pain; poor circulation in the legs or in general; dry or rough skin; a tendency toward anemia; and, for women, chronic problems in the sex organs.

When the stomach energy is excessive, the person tends to think too much. He or she usually has an enormous ambition, or appetite for life, but cannot fulfill it and thus is frustrated. Such people are chronically unsatisfied. They can be emotionally extreme—either cold and lacking in affection or overly affectionate. They are big eaters, but they are in a hurry and lack appreciation for their food. They are constantly striving, without feeling they have reached the goal. They tend to be neurotic.

THE HEART MERIDIAN

The heart and small intestine are the meridians associated with the experience of joy.

When the Heart Energy Is Depleted, or Kyo

Depleted heart energy causes heart disease, palpitations, angina pectoris, tension in hara, and sweaty palms. The person with depleted heart energy is easily fatigued, usually has a coated tongue, and has tension in the solar plexus. He or she is at high risk for a heart attack.

Weak heart energy causes mental fatigue, shock, nervous tension, chronic stress, timidity, poor appetite for food and for life, lack of memory, deficiency or complete lack of will, and chronic disappointment.

When the Heart Energy Is Excessive, or Jitsu

Excess energy in the heart causes a sensation of tension and tightness in the heart and chest area. Again, the person with excess heart energy has sweaty palms, a constant need to clear the throat, skin sensitivity, shoulder and arm pain, nervous stomach, and palpitations. There may be a pulling sensation in the tongue and an overall stiffness in the body.

Excess heart energy causes chronic tension, stress, restlessness, inability to relax, and a need to be distracted from the discomfort the heart is suffering. The person with excess heart energy is always doing something with his or her hands—adjusting the pants or shirt, touching the face, playing with the hair. This person tires easily and has little endurance; tends to stammer; has chronic stiffness in the solar plexus; and is constantly thirsty. He or she has bouts of hysteria, laughing or crying wildly at the least incentive.

THE SMALL-INTESTINE MERIDIAN

The small intestine is responsible for taking nutrition out of food and making it available to the bloodstream. The abstract role of the small intestine is profound. From the gross, or unrefined, matter, the small intestine draws out what is essential and makes it available to us to sustain life. There is no more important role in our own lives than to see what is of value in our environment and make use of it.

The quality of our blood—that is, the extent to which it receives adequate nutrition—depends on our diet and the functioning of the small intestine. If our diet is depleted in nutrition, or we consume a diet rich in fat and cholesterol, which coat the tiny villi of the small intestine, we will be unable to draw sufficient nutrients from our food. Consequently, the cells will be undernourished. They will have to leach nutrients from neighboring tissues, including bones and teeth.

In addition, the small intestine absorbs iron from our food, which helps carry oxygen to cells throughout the body. When iron levels are low, the oxygen-carrying capacity of the blood is diminished. Therefore, our ability to absorb adequate iron depends on the healthy functioning of the small intestine.

When the Small-Intestine Energy Is Depleted, or Kyo

When a person has depleted small-intestine energy, nutrient absorption is poor. The person may suffer to some degree from malnutrition. There is a greater likelihood of anemia and chronic fatigue, especially in the hips and legs. There may be lower-back problems and insufficient strength in hara. There will likely be blood stagnation in the small intestine itself, which, if not corrected, will only lead to a worsening of health in the future.

A weak small-intestine condition contributes to other types of digestive problems, including constipation and appendicitis. In women, small-intestine disorders lead to chronic menstrual problems, including premenstrual syndrome, and ovarian pain and cysts. Intestinal disorders of all kinds tend to create headaches. Depletion of the small-intestine energy often leads to migraines.

The person who suffers from a weakened small intestine tends to think too much. Such people suffer from anxiety; they tend to control their emotions with their minds, but experience a lack of joy and sometimes deep sadness.

Weak small-intestine energy often lies at the root of a person's inability to make the most of his or her talents. People with weak small-intestine energy often sense their inherent abilities and opportunities in their work, but are unable to fully exploit them. This causes much frustration and deep-seated self-doubt.

When the Small-Intestine Energy Is Excessive, or Jitsu

When a person has excessive small-intestine energy, he or she often has stiffness in the cervical vertebrae and solar plexus, especially in the morning. There is also a coldness in hara, due to lack of blood circulation to the lower organs. Such people also have poor circulation to the extremities, cold hands and feet, and chronic constipation that can alternate with diarrhea. They may need to urinate frequently, and may have other bladder problems and, in women, ovarian pain.

People with excessive energy in the small intestine tend to have strong determination and an ability to finish what they begin. They are restless, overworked, and eat too rapidly. They withhold their emotions, often to their own detriment, and have trouble relaxing. They are highly ambitious, but often fail to appreciate their accomplishments.

THE BLADDER MERIDIAN

The bladder and kidneys are related organs, according to both Oriental and Western medicine. As with the kidneys, the emotion associated with the bladder is fear. The bladder influences the hormonal system, pituitary gland, and autonomic nervous system. It has a direct bearing on the sex organs and urinary tract.

When the Bladder Energy Is Depleted, or Kyo

The person with bladder weakness often suffers from frequency of urination, faulty bladder control, and nervous tension. Such people have poor circulation, tightness in the legs, and coolness along the spine and buttocks. (This is where the bladder meridian runs—down the back, across the buttocks, down both legs to the feet, and terminating in the small toe.) They may well have problems in the sex organs. Bladder weakness often causes night sweats.

People with weak bladder energy are usually timid and nervous. They harbor many fears, are highly sensitive, and complain chronically.

When the Bladder Energy Is Excessive, or Jitsu

Those with excessive energy in the bladder may have stiffness in the neck. Such people often suffer from migraine headaches, especially brought on by suppressed fears. There is a heaviness in the eyes and head, tightness in the backs of the legs, frequency of urination, and often an inflamed prostate gland. The autonomic nervous system may be strained as well.

People with excess bladder energy worry over trivial details. They are nervous and restless and overly sensitive. Like those with kidney trouble, they also suffer from a fear of imminent disaster.

THE GALLBLADDER MERIDIAN

The gallbladder and liver are complementary organs. Bile acids are stored in the liver and distributed to the intestines, where they help to break down foods, especially fatty foods. As I mentioned earlier, bile acids are buffered by cholesterol in the gallbladder. If the cholesterol level becomes excessive, the bile acids will not be able to keep the cholesterol in solution; they will crystallize and form gallstones, which become extremely painful.

When the Gallbladder Energy Is Depleted, or Kyo

People whose gallbladder energy is depleted have a lack of bile, poor digestion, and a tendency to diarrhea. They sleep poorly and have dizziness, excess mucus in the eyes, pale complexions, acidic stomach, and discomfort on the right side of the solar plexus.

Psychologically, these people tend to be repressed and angry. Their anger often surfaces as rage. They tend to suffer nervous tension. Such people can be timid, easily frightened, and lacking in determination. They dream of accomplishing things, but often have neither the will nor the courage to make their dreams reality.

When the Gallbladder Energy Is Excessive, or Jitsu

In people whose gallbladder energy is excessive, there is a lack of sleep, much thinking and planning, and discomfort and even pain on the right side of the solar plexus. These people may have a loss of appetite, a yellowish coloration in the whites of the eyes, and a pressure in the eyes that sometimes causes them to bulge with emotion. They often have a bitter taste in the mouth, shoulder pain, stiff muscles, migraine headaches, constipation, mucous stagnation, excessive intake of sweets, and a distaste for sour foods.

Psychologically, these people tend to assume too much responsibility for work; they push too hard, pay too much attention to details, and are easily upset, impatient, and always in a hurry.

THE HEART CONSTRICTOR MERIDIAN

The heart constrictor meridian runs from the armpit down the arm to the tip of the middle finger. In Oriental medicine, the heart constrictor meridian provides supplemental energy to the heart and circulation, and the cardiac sac. Since it assists circulation, the heart constrictor energy is partly responsible for providing adequate oxygen and nutrition to cells throughout the body.

Problems related to heart constrictor energy are similar to those associated with the heart.

When the Heart Constrictor Energy Is Depleted, or Kyo

The person with weak heart constrictor energy has difficulty swallowing, is prone to sore throats and tonsillitis, palpitations, low blood pressure, discomfort and even pain in the chest and rib cage. Such people may have shortness of breath and a squeezing sensation in the chest.

Psychologically, such people are restless and absent-minded; they have trouble sleeping.

When the Heart Constrictor Energy Is Excessive, or Jitsu

People with excessive heart constrictor energy suffer from strong palpitations, high blood pressure, dizziness, and chronic fatigue. They have poor circulation, stiffness in the solar plexus and hara, and some pain in the stomach. They can have general tightness in the hands and palms;

coated tongue; and some digestive problems, including spastic bowel.

Excess heart constrictor energy causes restlessness, nervousness, and a turning away from emotional issues or anything having to do with the heart.

THE TRIPLE HEATER MERIDIAN

The triple heater meridian runs up the arm from the fourth finger to the shoulder, up the neck, and around the top of the ear to the temple, connecting three energy centers.

When the Triple Heater Energy Is Depleted, or Kyo

The person with depleted triple heater energy is highly sensitive to changes in temperature and humidity; he or she easily catches cold, has tired eyes and sensitive skin, is often allergic to pollen and other antigens, suffers from tightness in the chest and hara, has low blood pressure, and suffers pain in the back of the head and in the temples.

Psychologically, such people have many obsessions. Their imbalance is often the result of too much pampering in childhood. They are highly sensitive in general.

When the Triple Heater Energy Is Excessive, or Jitsu

People with excessive energy in the triple heater tend to suffer from lymphatic inflammation and nasal mucus. They are prone to accidents and have poor circulation, itchy skin, tightness in the chest, heaviness in the legs, and inflammation in the gums, mouth, and womb.

Excessive energy in the triple heater makes people extremely cautious, hypersensitive, ever on the alert. These people dislike changes in humidity and temperature, and are easily fatigued.

One of the best ways to diagnose another person using the Five Transformations and meridian diagnosis is by diagnosing the voice. Simply by talking to a person, you can ascertain much about his or her current psychology. Let's examine voice diagnosis, using the information I've just given you.

DIAGNOSING THE VOICE

In Oriental diagnosis, we say that the heart is the master of the voice, meaning that the heart controls the use of the voice. We all know this on some level. When we are in love, we sing; when angry, we scream; when sad, we cry; when content, we hum. While these are generalizations, we can easily recognize that our emotions dramatically affect the way we use our voices.

In Oriental medicine, the emotions associated with the heart are joy and hysteria—one a positive expression, the other an imbalanced one. Joy in the voice can be heard as a laughing quality. A person may be discussing a very mundane topic, but if the heart is strong or dominant, we can still hear a happy bounce in the words, indicating a strong, happy nature. As for recognizing hysteria in the voice, you don't have to be an Oriental diagnostician to do that.

Just as the heart is the master of the voice, the kidneys are its roots. A voice that comes from the kidneys, that is, from low in the body, is deep, rich, and reverberating. A high voice, especially in a man, indicates some type of kidney weakness. Check the rest of the face—especially the area below the eyes—to see what the problem might be with the kidneys.

The emotion associated with the kidneys is fear. Often we can hear a specific emotion in the voice—a fearfulness, for example, or trembling. Listen to the voice to see whether there is a degree of fear. A person who speaks forthrightly and directly, with confidence in his voice, has strong kidney energy. Occasionally you detect a watery quality in the voice. This is not merely the presence of mucus, though you will encounter this quality as well. What I mean by "watery" is a weak voice that seems to bear a certain teariness, a melancholic quality. Chronic melancholia is often caused by a kidney imbalance.

Listen to the direction of the voice as the person speaks. Does the voice go downward in a serious manner, becoming less emotional and graver, or does it rise, becoming more emotional and out of control? Does the voice remain a monotone? Or is it irregular, a series of hills and valleys? The tendency will tell you much about the person's inner condition. A grave quality that runs to grief reveals a problem in the lungs or large intestine.

The lungs are known as the gateway of the voice, meaning that they provide the air necessary to make the larynx function. The emotion associated with the lungs is grief. You can easily detect grief as sadness or deep emotional pain. Grief is closely associated with anger—in fact, grief will give rise to anger in many people.

Anger in the voice reveals an imbalance in the liver. An angry voice is very easy to discern; immediately, you know there is a liver problem.

If you hear excessive sympathy—a "poor little me" or "poor little you" quality—in the voice, you should question the strength of the spleen. Ask the person whether he or she eats a lot of sugar or drinks wine, both of which injure the spleen. Such a person should eat more squash and round vegetables, like eggplant, and foods rich in minerals, all of which strengthen the spleen. (See chapter 9 for healing foods.)

• • •

Life is energy. Without it, nothing moves, nothing rests. Without energy, matter is inanimate. When we see energy, we are seeing spirit. Each spirit is a unique manifestation of the Great Spirit, Tao. Therefore, we must not make negative judgments about anyone. Instead, we must marvel at the infinite creativity of Tao, or God. As Oriental diagnosticians, our only desire is to facilitate the movement of energy within ourselves and each person we encounter—to bring forth our own inner being, as well as the inner being of those around us. By acquiring this wonderful knowledge, we have it in our power to serve such a purpose: to move energy in the direction in which it already wants to go. What a great way to live!

4

Hara

"HARA" LITERALLY MEANS "VITAL CULTURE" or "vital center of life." It means the center of gravity. This center of gravity, however, must be seen in a much broader sense. Hara is the point of balance for our physical, mental, emotional, and spiritual life. When one is said to be centered, balanced, and focused, one is in touch with hara.

In the Orient, the meaning of hara is so extensive, so all-permeating, that to suggest that it can be summed up in a single phrase or short set of phrases would be misleading. Cultivation of and communion with hara is a lifelong endeavor for the Japanese. All martial arts, all cultural arts (including painting and music), all spiritual disciplines, and all business transactions are performed—with greater or lesser success—from one's hara. Hara is the center of the self. It is the spiritual root of your life. Just as the roots of a tree bury themselves in the earth to draw nourishment, hara is the root from which you draw your power and connectedness to the universal energy. Hara is your spiritual umbilical chord. Universal energy flows into your being through hara.

In his wonderful book, *Hara: The Vital Center of Man* (George Allen & Unwin, 1962), Karlfried Graf von Durckheim points out that we humans are always suspended between the archetypal poles of heaven and earth, space and time. These poles pull at us from their specific vantage points: heaven, urging us toward higher ideals and the ultimate communion with the spirit; earth, drawing us into desire for accomplishment, power, wealth, and longevity. The duality of heaven and earth is played out in our limited space-time existence on earth.

This duality creates an overwhelming set of tensions within us, each pulling in its own direction. A man or woman's life is a struggle to integrate these archetypes. We may fool ourselves into thinking such realms exist outside of ourselves, but in fact heaven and earth are realms within our own consciousness. Therefore, life itself is an attempt to balance and integrate these two antagonistic and complementary poles.

Often we give in to one or the other, forsaking the earth for heaven, or letting go of heaven for the overwhelming temptations of the earth. Where is balance and integration? The answer is in hara. Hara is the way of integration. It is the true center of self, where the duality of life is brought into harmony. At our own spiritual center, hara, there is peace and balance. Therefore, the Oriental cultivates an attitude that attempts to make every movement and action spring from his or her hara.

As the vital center, hara is the source of health, personal vitality, and endurance. When a person acts from hara, his or her movements are effortless. He or she is borne along by the infinite power of the universe, one with the Tao.

While a discussion of hara can reach lofty heights, hara itself is eminently practical in its application to life.

Every physical object, including our own bodies, has a center of gravity from which balance is achieved. If the center of gravity is low, the object in question remains solidly fixed on any surface. It cannot be easily moved. If the center of gravity is high, the object becomes unbalanced and can easily be moved or toppled. Things that are top-heavy fall easily. Things that are bottom-heavy do not.

In the human body, hara occupies the general area between the solar plexus and the pubic bone. Its specific root lies at a point between the navel and the pubic bone. This is why Orientals traditionally refer to a person with a strong hara as having guts. Those with a developed hara have courage and the capacity to endure.

Hara is seen as our second brain; it is also called the "little brain." Directly behind the general area of hara, just below the solar plexus at the spine, is a bundle of nerves that represents the greatest concentration of nerves outside the brain. This concentration of nerves is responsible for many of the movements of the lower part of the body. When you cut off a chicken's head, for example, the chicken's body continues to run around, though it has no brain to direct its movements. It is the little brain, the autonomic nervous system, that directs the chicken's actions. The dinosaur had a huge body and a little head with a tiny brain. Its brain was far too small to carry on all the functions of its great body. Instead, its nervous system directed many of its body movements.

It is the same with people. Many functions go on involuntarily within us: the beating of our hearts, for example, and our breathing. We can consciously control our breathing, but for the most part it goes on without our control.

We can begin learning hara diagnosis by recognizing how we and others breathe, that is, where we hold our breath once we draw it into our bodies. Do you draw your breath into the lower part of your body, the stomach and lower intestinal area, or do you breathe mostly from your upper chest?

When you breathe deeply into this lower area, you nourish and develop your hara. As your hara becomes stronger, you feel more relaxed, capable, and confident. Those whose breath is more shallow, that is, remains in the upper part of the chest, are uniformly more nervous, emotional, uncertain, and insecure. Numerous scientific studies have established this as fact.

People whose breathing is shallow do not realize that breath is ki and that excess ki stimulates the energy center at the heart. When this energy center, known in the East as the heart chakra, becomes overly excited, the person's body is thrown off balance. His or her emotions become excited and out of control. Nervous tension increases. The person understandably lacks confidence, knowing that his or her energies are not stable. (To strengthen hara, do the exercise explained below on a daily basis. In no time, you will feel your hara become more powerful, and you will become more confident and secure.)

Shallow breathing raises our center of gravity to the chest, where the energies become excited. Indeed, when our emotional center is unstable, it takes little to knock us off balance or make us upset. The very word "upset" describes precisely what I mean.

By recognizing how you and others breathe, you begin to understand the strength of your and their haras and psychological natures.

When we are strong in hara, our actions are grounded and we remain balanced, no matter what turmoil may exist around us.

The West has cultivated the energy centers, or chakras, above hara. This is why all Western soldiers are told to stand at attention with their stomachs in and their chests out. The energy is lifted up from hara and into the chest. The lower abdomen becomes tight and retracted. This prevents the breath from going deeply into the center of hara. Such posture is unnatural for humans. It is much more comfortable and stable to let the energy rest lower in the abdomen and let our actions flow from this point.

In Japan, even the simplest action is directed from hara. For example, when we cut wood, we pull the saw toward us in a downward motion, using our body weight to draw the saw through the wood. The center of gravity is in hara, and the motion is downward. This allows us to use a very narrow blade, since there is no downward tension on the blade. (It can be as flexible as a ribbon, as long as it will cut. A narrow

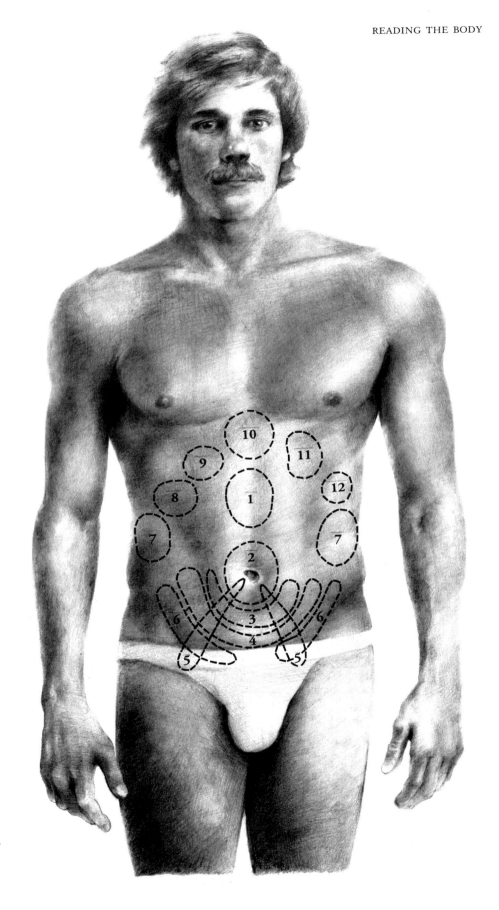

Meridians: (1) heart constrictor,
(2) spleen, (3) kidney,
(4) bladder, (5) small intestine,
(6) large intestine,
(7) lung, (8) liver, (9) gallbladder,
(10) heart, (11) stomach,
(12) triple heater.

blade makes a narrow cut and allows carpentry joints to fit closely together—doors and windows in Japan fit tightly without the use of nails. In the West, wood is cut by pushing the saw downward. The center of activity is from the shoulder down through the arm. In this posture, the wood offers maximum resistance to the blade and the body. Therefore, the blade must be thick and the body must work twice as hard.

In Japan, all action is more likely to pull, rather than push. If you want to understand Japanese culture—the martial arts, shiatsu, dance, cooking, anything—you must understand this fact.

The Oriental martial art of judo is based on the same notion. You use the advancing energy of your opponent to disarm him. You actually allow your opponent to advance and then direct his energy away from you. This is done by pulling the opponent in the direction in which you want him to go. You can do this because he has initiated the advance.

In negotiations, the Japanese do not push other people. Instead, they are constantly retreating and, in the process, pulling their adversaries toward them.

I am blessed to have as my good friend Henry Kissinger, the U.S. Secretary of State under President Nixon. Dr. Kissinger and I love to talk about the differences between East and West. Once he was the guest of honor at a party at my school in New York, and he gave a

In Ohashiatsu, don't push; pull and support.

little talk about the way the Japanese negotiate. Kissinger described a meeting he had with Japanese dignitaries in which he put forth an American proposal. The Japanese leaders uttered, "Yes, yes," after every one of his suggestions, and by the conclusion of the meeting he thought he had made a deal. When he returned to the United States, he discovered that the Japanese had disagreed with everything he had said. Kissinger protested, "You said 'Yes' after every one of my proposals."

The Japanese replied, "What we meant was 'Yes, yes, we heard you.' " By retreating, the Japanese attempt to pull the opponent toward the Japanese position.

This cultivation of hara by the Japanese corresponds to their height. I am very short, only five feet one inch. In my classes, I ask one of my taller male students to stand up next to me. The student is usually six feet or taller, and we make a very humorous couple. Sometimes I ask a female student to come to the front of the room, too, so that on the right is a very tall man and on the left a very tall woman and in the middle the very short Ohashi.

Then I suggest that we all three sit down on the floor and stretch our legs out. Sitting down, we are remarkably similar in height. There is very little difference in the level of our heads, though our legs are extremely different in length.

The difference in our heights is not in our torsos but our legs. Their torsos are on stilts, I like to say. This means that our centers of gravity are at different heights, and that my center of gravity is actually the lowest because my torso sits on the shortest legs.

Let's begin learning to diagnose another person's hara. First, and most important, you must achieve the right attitude toward the person before you. You are looking for his or her spirit, his or her character. You are searching for tendencies within the inner nature. You are feeling this person's energy body, the spirit. A person feels very vulnerable at hara. Each of us seeks to protect this part of the body, because intuitively we know it is the source of our life. Consequently, no one wants to be touched here unless it is by someone they trust.

Ask your friend to lie down on his or her back, preferably on a futon on the floor. Sit next to your friend and lower your own hara to the floor, or as close as you can make it.

Before you even extend your hands to touch your friend, meditate. Clear your mind of all thoughts. Become receptive to the gentle vibrations of the universe. Ask your friend to take long, deep breaths. Align your breathing with your friend's.

You must become very yin now. Let go of all aggressive or yang tendencies. Become a mother to this person. My teacher, Master Shizuto Masunaga, used to tell us that when diagnosing and massaging hara, we must become a mother with a samurai's mind. That means that

In Ohashiatsu, bring your own hara toward the other person: don't press; pull.

while we are eminently gentle, we are at the same time focused, directed, and alert.

Let all the tension drain from your shoulders, arms, and hands. Do not tense your fingertips or allow any nervous energy to infiltrate your hands. Make sure your hands are warm and soft. If you are not relaxed, resume deep breathing with your friend. If your hands are cold, rub them until the circulation warms them. You can run warm water over your hands or rub them with salt before a treatment; this will warm them and give them a good, strong ki. Relax your face. Do not wear a severe expression on your face, but appear gentle and reassuring. Make sure there is no draft in your environment. You want your friend to be as comfortable as possible.

Ask your friend to part his or her legs just slightly and then raise them so that the feet remain on the floor and the knees are bent upward. This will open or expose the hara. Now the stomach muscles will be loose and flexible. If the legs are straight, closed or crossed, hara is also closed. Crossing of the legs on the floor is a natural protective measure, but you want your friend to relax and to trust you.

You are about to place your hands on the abdomen and explore the area between the rib cage and the pubic bone. You will feel varying degrees of tension and laxness. You will be exploring the specific areas shown in the illustration to diagnose the condition of these organs.

Always use two hands on the abdomen, never one. Use your hands in a coordinated manner so that one hand explores while the other reassures. One hand is yang; it gently probes the area in question, discovering its resistances or weaknesses. The other hand relaxes, smooths the energies, and assures your friend of your healing intentions. That is precisely what your massage must do: heal by restoring balance to the body. You are moving ki, bringing it to places where it is deficient, taking it away from places where it is excessive.

As I mentioned earlier, the hara is both a general area of the abdomen and a specific point below the navel. The general hara area reveals the condition of the specific organs of the abdomen. You are not always feeling the organ itself, but the places where energy from specific organs accumulates. These are acupuncture points on energy meridians; they reveal the condition of the organs.

Let's begin with the right side of the body, directly below the rib cage. We will be moving incrementally upward from just below the rib cage to the solar plexus and then downward along the rib cage to the left side of the body. We will then explore the mid-region of the stomach and lower areas: the left, right and center of the abdomen, just above the pubic bone.

The area on the right side of the body just below the right side of the rib cage (at about nine o'clock on the stomach area) reveals the condition of the right lung. If it is tight or tense, like a clenched fist, we say that it is *jitsu*. That means that there is tension in the lung and that the organ needs relaxation or sedation. Perhaps there is congestion or stagnant ki. If the area is limp or lacks vitality, we say it is *kyo*. We will need to tone and strengthen the organs that are kyo.

Next, move upward to the ten o'clock position on the abdomen and feel the liver. Again, explore the organ to see if it is jitsu or kyo. At eleven o'clock is the gallbladder. Make the same mental notations. Directly at twelve o'clock, at the solar plexus, is the heart area. Gently touch the area and note the energy.

To the left of the heart is the stomach point; to the left of the stomach is the triple heater point. The triple heater is the name given to the three energy centers, or chakras, of the abdomen: the heart, stomach, and hara. Directly below the heart point is another heart point, called the heart governor, which is a meridian that nourishes the heart. Directly below the navel is the spleen, and below that the kidneys. At eight o'clock on the abdomen is the large-intestine point. At seven o'clock is the small-intestine area. At six o'clock is the bladder. At five o'clock is the small intestine; at four o'clock is the large intestine.

As you probe each of these points, bring your whole energy into the exploration. Move your body over your friend's, so that you are probing deeply, gently, and carefully.

Check your friend's face to see whether anything you are doing is painful. As you apply your hands, ask your friend questions regarding the information you are receiving from your massage. "Is there any digestive problem?" you may ask, if the large- or small-intestine area seems unbalanced.

When you have made your assessment, you may continue to massage gently, redirecting the energies accordingly and making dietary or life-style recommendations when you are finished. If the hara is weak, suggest the following exercise:

To cultivate stability, balance, and confidence, you should practice daily deep-breathing exercises and meditation. Visualize your hara as a point of light just below the navel. Breathe deeply into hara, while visualizing this light growing more powerful and alive with every breath. See the energy of hara expand in all directions to infuse your being with energy, vitality, and life. Continue breathing ki into your vital center. With each breath, visualize hara being nourished and enriched so that the vital center grows more powerful with every inhalation. Finish the exercise by taking a long inhalation into hara and holding it for five seconds. Exhale and relax. Draw another breath in and hold it again in hara for five seconds. Relax. Do this for several minutes. This is a wonderful grounding exercise.

In the art of both East and West, the great spiritual teachers, such as Jesus, the Buddha, or Lao-tzu, are always depicted with beautifully developed haras. Their lower abdomens are rounded, full, and strong. This suggests highly developed people, capable of great deeds, essentially because their vital centers are anchored in the universal energy— God, Tao, or the Great Spirit—which they are able to manifest and channel for the good of some larger purpose.

5

The Back

I AM A GREAT FAN OF THE BALLET, and one of my favorites is *Swan Lake*. I have seen many different productions of *Swan Lake* and have come to appreciate the various styles individual ballerinas bring to the lead role. One of the crucial tests of whether a ballerina can really bring across the role of Odette comes toward the end of the ballet, when Odette must communicate her grief at having to forsake the human world and return to the world of swans. Some ballerinas attempt to show the anguish of this moment on their faces, arms, and legs. I am no dance critic, of course, but as a fan of the ballet, I have come to truly appreciate the ballerina who can communicate her grief not only with her face and the movements of her body, but also with her back. The great ballerinas somehow manage to reveal their suffering in their entire bodies, especially in their shoulders and backs. The shoulders arch forward; the back communicates the enormous weight of despair. The great ballerina conveys the emotion of this moment completely, and we, in the audience, are moved.

In Japan, when a person is truly sad, we say his shoulders are crying. Now that's sad. That's truly crying. Sometimes we say the opposite; we say his back is laughing, meaning that he is really happy. The reason we use these expressions is that the Japanese do not show much emotion, but when a person suffers deep pain, or expresses great happiness, he reveals his emotion in his posture, especially in his back.

All people are very front-conscious. When you think of your appearance, you think of your front. You meet the world with your front;

the word "confront" says it all. Consequently, we dress up our fronts with jewelry, ties, interesting clothing, shiny shoes, makeup, and fancy hairdos. You cannot do much with your back; it cannot be manipulated very much, nor is there much to adorn.

Thus, I believe the back is more honest. It is more revealing of the inner you.

In human evolution, the back has gone from a horizontal position to a vertical one. Obviously, this change from horizontal to vertical altered us in every way—physically, psychologically, and spiritually.

We can see some of the changes this evolution in posture brought about in the development of children. As infants, we move our limbs laterally in what is called the homologous position, like an alligator or other reptile. The next stage of movement is homolateral or cross-patterning—that is, we crawl by coordinating the movements of the right arm and left leg, and the left arm and right leg. This is the pattern of all four-legged animals. Eventually, we stand up and walk. This completes the entire evolutionary cycle of life on earth. We have now evolved from a single cell to a multicellular organism in the watery world of our mother's womb (duing which time we actually resemble a fish) to birth onto the land. At this point, we take on the movements that belong to the stages of evolution explained above—from reptile to four-legged animal, and finally to human being.

Each stage is essential to proper brain, muscle, and nerve development. Cervical vertebrae—the vertebrae of the neck—develop as a baby learns to lift its head. Crawling is the best exercise in preparation for walking. If a baby crawls or walks too soon, there can be problems in bone, nerve, muscle, and brain development. An example of this is the child who walks too soon and develops weak hips and later a problem with pigeon-toes and knock-knees. This person may also develop lower-back ache early in life. He or she stood up before the body was ready. The hips, bones, and muscle development were not ready to support such a step.

Interestingly, even as adults we repeat this same evolutionary cycle. In bed each night, we take on the posture of an infant in the womb; when we wake, we stretch (homologous movement); we crawl out of bed (cross-patterning) and then finally stand up. At night, we repeat the process in reverse.

To diagnose the back, we must understand the spine. The principal parts of the spine that we will be concentrating on are the twenty-four vertebrae forming the central part of the spine. From the top of the spine, these vertebrae are the seven cervical, twelve thoracic, and five lumbar vertebrae. Between thoracic vertebrae five and six is the center of the back.

Between each pair of vertebrae is a cushion or disk which absorbs

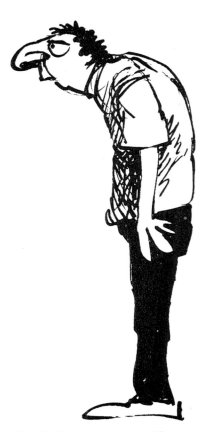

Your back represents your life and character.

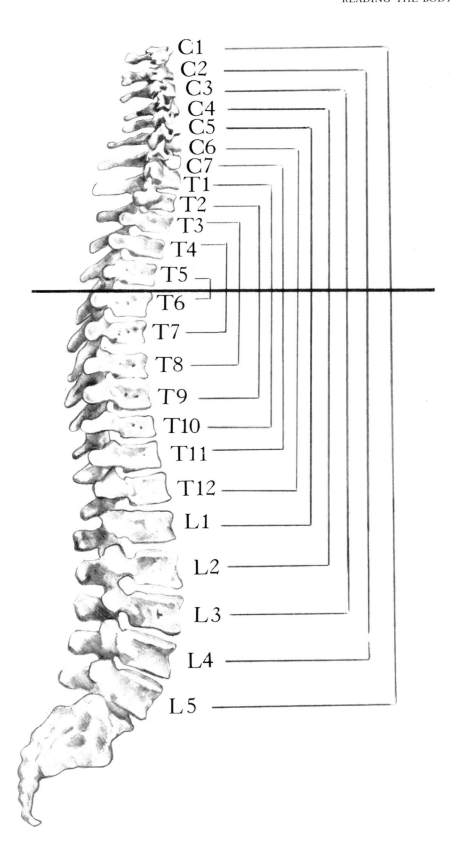

C1
C2
C3
C4
C5
C6
C7
T1
T2
T3
T4
T5
T6
T7
T8
T9
T10
T11
T12
L1
L2
L3
L4
L5

Dividing line between thoracic 5
and thoracic 6.

and disperses the shock of walking and running. Sometimes this disk moves or slips (a condition called a slipped disk), pinching the nerves between the vertebrae.

The vertebrae of the spine have an opposite and complementary relationship with each other: the top of the spine relates to the bottom, and vice versa. If there is pain at the top of the spine, the injury likely occurred at the bottom. If there is pain at the bottom of the spine, the injury likely occurred at the neck. If your friend has pain in the lower back, ask whether he or she has ever experienced whiplash or an injury to the third or fourth cervical vertebra.

In the same way, problems with the jaw or teeth are often caused by too much tension in the lower back. Sometimes children grind their teeth while sleeping. This might indicate problems with the kidneys or sex organs. Perhaps there is a problem with the parent of the opposite sex, causing energy to be trapped in the sex organs and giving rise to tension in the lower back area.

If your child grinds his or her teeth, do the following:

1. Change the child's pillow to one that is round and hard.
2. Have the child sleep on a firmer mattress or futon.
3. Have the child do exercises before bed to work off some tension.
4. Reestablish harmony with the parent of the opposite sex.

The opposite and complementary relationship between the vertebrae is especially important in diagnosing the origin of back problems and treating the spine. You do not want to touch the area where there is pain. Instead, go to the opposite end of the spine and gently massage the vertebrae. For example, if there is pain in the lower back, say the fifth lumbar vertebra, gently apply your hands and soothe the area of the first and second cervical vertebrae. The opposite is also true: if there is pain in the neck, gently soothe the lumbar vertebrae to bring relief. (See the diagram for the corresponding vertebrae.) This is the case with all the vertebrae of the back.

I like to say in my classes that American people know this Oriental secret very well. They always refer to people who give them a pain in the neck as "pains in the ass."

There is always some distortion in the back. To see just one of your own distortions, fold your hands. Does your left thumb overlap your right thumb or vice versa? Try to reverse your folded hands so that the hand that is normally dominant is tucked under the one that is normally passive. It feels strange, doesn't it? Now go to a mirror and fold your hands naturally. Look in the mirror and check your shoulders. Normally, the shoulder that corresponds with the dominant thumb will be slightly higher than the submissive thumb: right thumb dominant, right shoulder higher. Ninety-five percent of people are noticeably unbalanced in this way.

Another way to see your imbalance is to close your eyes and walk in place. It is better to do this exercise in your room or in a place that is free of obstacles you can bump into. Walk in place for three or four minutes and then open your eyes. You will no longer be facing the same direction you were facing when you began. You will have turned, either clockwise or counterclockwise. If you moved to the right in a clockwise manner, your right side is dominant, and likely too contracted; if you moved to the left, your left side is dominant and too contracted. This means that the organs and muscles on the dominant side are too tense and tight, while the other side is expanded and loose. Various yoga routines—such as stretching postures and exercises—and massage can balance the extremes in your body.

Often I bring two of my students to the front of the classroom and ask them to walk in place with their eyes closed. They frequently set off in two different directions and wind up in very different parts of the room. The class has a lot of fun with this.

A person's unevenness often becomes a habit that is characteristic of the person. The actor Peter Falk is wonderful as the TV detective Lieutenant Columbo, partly because of the idiosyncratic way he walks and holds his body. His distortion is his trademark. If he lost his distortion, he'd stop being who he is.

Once a very famous singer-entertainer came to me for a treatment. She had a very pronounced left-right imbalance that caused her to hold the microphone and sing in a very characteristic way. It affected the way she danced and moved on stage. All of this became her trademark, as well as her personal habit.

I gave her a series of treatments that corrected the distortion. Unfortunately, once she was released from the imbalance she became terribly confused onstage. She no longer felt comfortable holding the microphone or singing in her characteristic poses. One night she called me in a fright.

"Ohashi," she said, "I've forgotten how to hold the microphone and dance. I'm lost out there. I want my imbalance back."

You may know some people like him.

The spine is very like a suspension bridge. It is delicately balanced and supported by all the elements that make up the entire structure—not merely the vertebrae, which might be seen as the bridge itself, but by all the other factors that make up the body, including the organs and the muscular and skeletal systems. If any one part becomes unbalanced, the spine can be affected. In other words, the spine is a delicate chain of bones that relies on many other elements within the body to maintain the integrity of its structure. This is why so many people suffer from

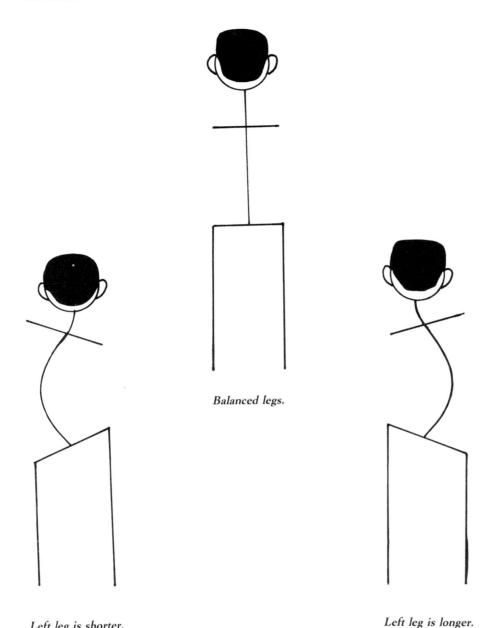

Balanced legs.

Left leg is shorter.   *Left leg is longer.*

backache—because our ways of life today cause imbalances throughout the body, which in turn often affect the spine.

There are three main causes of backache. The first is structural damage, caused by an accident, exercise routine, or some habit that results in misalignment of the vertebrae. Obviously, an accident or injury can cause the back to go out of alignment, resulting in back pain. You will have to see a doctor or chiropractor to determine the extent of the pain. Very often, exercise, chiropractic, Ohashiatsu or shiatsu massage can be helpful in controlling the pain and even correcting the damage done by an injury. But the injury must be accurately diagnosed by a physician or some other professional for you to know the correct treatment.

Exercise and various habits—posture or the way you walk, for example—can cause muscles to develop in an unbalanced way. One side of the body can be tense and tight, the other loose and expanded. This puts differing tensions on the vertebrae. One set of muscles pulls hard; the other is loose and relaxed.

Tennis is one of many games that reinforce the same imbalance every time you play. I am not criticizing tennis—it's a great game—but it requires one side of your body to perform an exaggerated movement in comparison with the other side. To compensate for this, you should do exercises that strengthen your off side. If you play a game like tennis and you are a right-handed player, you should do exercises designed to strengthen and coordinate your left side, too. It is very important that you do warm-up exercises before playing any game that has a left-right imbalance. If you go out and play before your body is loose and ready, you will cause one side of your body to be exercised at a much greater rate than the other, exaggerating the imbalance all the more.

Ohashiatsu, chiropractic, and shiatsu massage can harmonize the left-right imbalance and bring relief from the type of backache caused by such an imbalance.

The second cause of backache is an imbalance in the internal organs, especially the liver, gallbladder, heart, spleen, or kidneys. If an organ becomes swollen, too tight, or weak, the spine will be affected. For example, the liver can become swollen or expanded from eating too many sweets and drinking too much alcohol. As the organ swells, it pushes against the muscles and vertebrae and causes the spine to go out of alignment. The same can happen with the stomach, spleen, or gallbladder.

In addition, ki, or life force, becomes stagnant in these swollen or troubled organs, causing blockages of ki that prevent that particular part of the body from being adequately nourished with life force. If ki becomes weaker in the liver, all the muscles surrounding the liver and back become starved for ki. Consequently, the integrity of the body is diminished and there is inadequate ki to support the spine.

Most lower-back ache involves the kidneys, in one of a variety of ways. The kidneys often become weak from the diet and behavior patterns I outlined earlier. The weakened kidneys and the lower area fail to support that vital part of the back and spine. When the kidneys become blocked from fats, salt, cholesterol, and stress, the amount of ki that reaches the organs and lower back is diminished. This reduces the ki flow to the spine, causing degeneration in the vertebrae and the muscles that support the back. Gradually, degeneration takes place in the muscles, lower back, and spine, causing pain and the lower-back ache that is so common today.

The third cause of backache is emotion. Emotion can be seen as increased energy, or ki. Fear, anger, sympathy, grief, and happiness—these and other emotions possess various degrees of energy, depending on the intensity of the emotion. The body rejoices in or suffers through each of these states. In all cases, however, it must do something with the energy that results from our emotional lives. Often we place this energy in various organs or repress it in our shoulders or backs, where it accumulates in the form of tension and bunched muscles. Each of us has developed a habit of placing our tension in various parts of our bodies; our livers, stomachs, kidneys, shoulders, and backs are common places for stored tension. This tension distorts the organs and the body itself, and affects the spine.

Using the theory of the Five Transformations discussed in chapter 3, we can see which organs are most troubled by the type of emotion that dominates the person we are trying to help. If the emotion is anger, the liver and gallbladder are most troubled; if there is backache, it will likely be in the middle of the back. If the person is grieving or sad, the lungs and large intestine are most affected; the back pain is higher, just below the shoulders. If there is fear or melancholy, the kidneys are troubled; in this case, the lower back is affected and lower-back ache is usually the result. If there is too much sympathy or weakness of character, it is often the spleen that is troubled; check the middle of the back, on the left side, to see whether there is swelling and discomfort here. If the heart is troubled, the person can become overly emotional and even hysterical; the center of the back, in the area of the heart, can be affected.

In Oriental diagnosis, various points on the front and back of the body are known as Bo and Yu points. Bo points, found in the front of the body, are located on various meridians. Yu points are all aligned on the bladder meridian along the spinal column (see chart). In general, pain or discomfort in the Bo points indicates acute problems and needs immediate attention. Pain in any of the Yu points indicates a more chronic problem.

The accompanying chart reveals which organs are causing pain or discomfort in either the Bo or Yu points. If the pain is in front, it is a Bo point; if in back, it is a Yu point. Pain or discomfort in the upper part of the body (front or back), below the clavicle and above the heart area, is generally caused by a problem in the lungs. Pain in the center of the chest or back means a problem in the heart. Just below the heart area on the right side of the body is the liver and gallbladder area. On the left side is the stomach. In the center is the spleen. Just below the spleen area, on both the left and right sides of the body, is the kidney

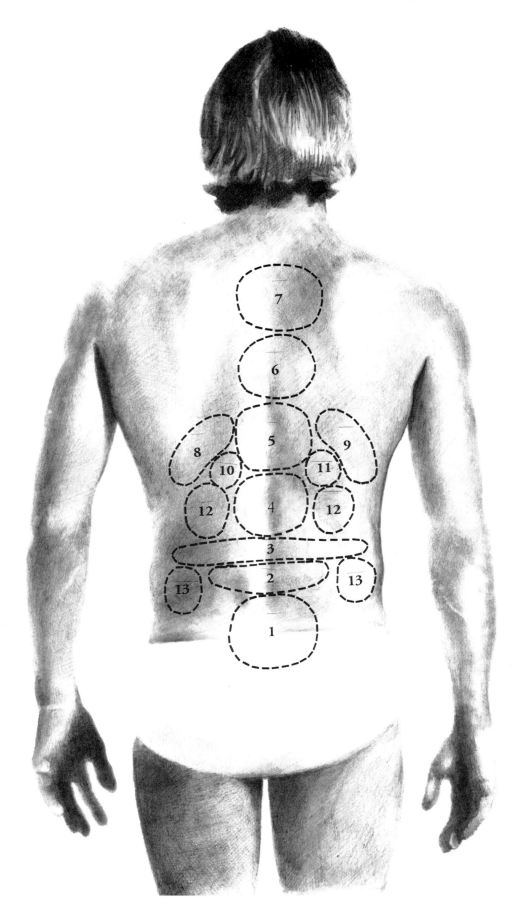

Meridians: (1) bladder,
(2) kidney, (3) small intestine,
(4) spleen, (5) heart constrictor,
(6) heart, (7) lung,
(8) stomach, (9) liver,
(10) triple heater,
(11) gallbladder,
(12) kidney, (13) large intestine.

band. Below the kidneys is the small intestine, and below that is the large intestine.

If there is back pain at any of these Yu points, the corresponding organs are suffering from chronic degeneration. A change of diet and exercise is called for. Ohashiatsu or some other exercise that balances ki should be part of the therapy.

If the pain is in the front, along the Bo points, the person should make immediate changes in diet, lifestyle, and exercise and should see a physician or trained healer to deal with the more immediate demands of the problem.

A form of diagnosis using Yu points, called scratching diagnosis, can be very effective. Ask the person to raise or remove his or her shirt so that the spine is exposed. Now, lightly run both your thumbnails along the left and right side of the spine along the bladder meridian, maintaining constant pressure so that the lines are not broken. Two light red lines should appear. If the lines are broken or white or gray, it indicates stagnation and lack of ki in the organs that correspond with that particular Yu point. For example, let's say that no red line appears in the center of the back on the right side. This would indicate some problem with the liver. Ask the person to stand up. Examine the area and compare its size and shape with the right side. Is it swollen or collapsed? This indicates some imbalance with the liver and the possible cause of the backache.

Hair often appears on various parts of the back and front of the body. Ideally, hair does not grow on the backs of humans. Hair growth in places that do not normally produce hair indicates blood stagnation, protein and fat accumulation, and excess mucus. Check to see where the hair is and note the corresponding Yu points and organs. If the hair is on the lung Yu point, it indicates a problem in the lungs, possibly from smoking, and the consumption of too many dairy products or other fatty foods. If there is hair on the lower part of the back, around or below the kidney area, it means there is too much mucus and blood stagnation in the reproductive organs and kidneys.

To diagnose someone from the back, you must sense the atmosphere of his or her back. There are so many postures, so many back shapes, that a whole book could be written about this aspect of the body. Let's examine some of the more common examples.

In general, there are backs that are bent forward, backs that are straight, and backs that are bent slightly backward.

People who walk with their upper bodies bent forward are more yang—that is, more aggressive, masculine, and self-initiating. They tend to be independent and quicker to get things done.

In Ohashiatsu the giver is the receiver, and the receiver is the giver. We are happy to be together.

The more noticeably bent forward a person is, the more stubborn he or she will be. Often, such people know what they want and are busy going after it. They have trouble listening to the advice of others. It is better to point such people in a general direction and let them take it from there. They aren't going to listen to you once they start moving, anyway. It takes a lot to knock such people off their course, or to change their thinking.

People whose bodies lean forward have trouble with the heart and intestines. The heart suffers from arteriosclerosis and lack of oxygen. The small intestine is too contracted, the large intestine too expanded. These people are often in a hurry and tend to eat on the run. Consequently, digestion is troubled. In general, they have trouble feeling adequately nourished on many levels—physically and psychologically. The function of the small intestine is to take in nourishment from the food and provide it to the bloodstream. The more abstract role of the small intestine is to take what is good and necessary from life and the environment and make it available to us as nourishment. When the small intestine is too contracted, it cannot take in sufficient nourishment from our diets, and its more abstract role of providing nourishment to our lives is also reduced. Thus we feel undernourished and underloved.

Such people should do exercises that stretch the arms and midsection outward and upward. These people should also eat more leafy green vegetables, which provide lots of oxygen and a more expansive energy to the body. They must learn to breathe deeply into the hara, or the lower parts of the body, and spend more time in nature. They must relax and feel the life force, or ki, enter the midsection of the body, causing expansion and relaxation.

Some people walk with their backs hunched up. Their shoulders are bunched and heaving forward. Such people are aggressive and poised for violence. It doesn't take much to set them off. They are actually creating conflict wherever they go. Their bodies reflect their thinking; they are constantly on the alert for trouble. There is considerable tension in the shoulders and spine, indicating trouble in the lungs and large intestines. There is much repressed anger and rage in these organs. Whole grains, especially brown rice, leafy green vegetables, and grated gingerroot on vegetables and in soups are recommended. Also, these people should enjoy plenty of physical exercise to let off steam and feel relaxed.

Some people—especially many women—walk with a very straight back. (This could be from wearing high-heeled shoes.) A straight back is a good sign. It reveals a principled and upright attitude toward the world. When you see a person with a straight back walking down the street, check to see where his or her center of gravity is. Is it high—in the heart or slightly lower in the solar plexus—or is it low, in the abdomen? You can tell where the center of gravity is by checking the shoulders. Shoulders that are pulled back (thus thrusting the chest forward) and set high show a higher center of gravity. Shoulders that are relaxed tend to sit comfortably in the middle of the body. Consequently, the weight of the body naturally falls to the hara.

A straight back with a high center of gravity shows a principled nature but a tendency toward excessive emotion. When the center of gravity is in the heart, the breathing is shallow and the person easily becomes emotional. Such a person may lack the will and drive to see his or her grander dreams to fruition.

The more the spine arches backward, the greater the tendency toward elitism and pride. Such a person holds himself or herself aloof from the world and too easily becomes critical of others.

The person whose back is straight and whose center of gravity is low possesses principles and strong will. The head sits evenly on the shoulders; the shoulders are relaxed and even. The weight of the upper body seems to rest on the hips, and yet there is no stress on the legs.

This is an integrated personality. He or she has determination and a clear-sighted view of the world. Such people are not likely to be Pollyannas, but realists whose ideals are still high. These people likely have high ambitions and can be counted on to carry out their tasks.

In terms of actual strength, many regard the back as the strongest part of the human body. But for a growing number of people the back is getting weaker and more painful every day. The reason is simple. Despite its great strength, the back is the place where the interdependence of the body is most obvious. It is indeed a suspension bridge, the place where many organs and muscles converge to create health or illness. Throw one set of organs or muscles out of balance and you have a lopsided bridge—and plenty of pain. Reestablish balance and harmony among the organs and muscles and you have a back that can bear the weight of the world, and do it joyfully.

6

The Hands and Arms

THE HANDS ARE AMONG THE MOST BEAUTIFUL and most important of human possessions. When we humans stood up, we freed our hands from the job of walking. We then began using them to perform more advanced chores. But it was the development of the opposable thumb that truly set us free. When we developed an opposable thumb, we were given the power to handle and manipulate the physical world. Everything from holding a pen to grasping a hammer—to say nothing of the creation of both instruments—was made possible by the gift of an opposable thumb.

We have created great edifices all over the world—and everything has been done by our hands. Hands are associated with creation. In Michelangelo's masterpiece on the ceiling of the Sistine Chapel, God— the source of creation—extends His hand to Adam. With this gesture, God bestows a measure of divinity on Adam by giving him the power of creativity.

What we envision with our minds is created with our hands. Therefore, the hands and the brain have long been seen as complementary. The brain envisions the world; the hands make the vision a reality.

The use of the hands is usually affected when a person suffers a stroke. As the brain capacity diminishes, so, too, does the use of our hands. This is revealed also in people suffering from senility. In Japan, origami, the art of paper folding, is used in rest homes and convalescent centers to help older people avoid senility and maintain mental alertness.

Conversely, children who use their fingers a lot develop their brains more rapidly. This is especially true of children who practice musical instruments that demand finger dexterity, such as the piano. Brain and nervous system development is enhanced.

People use their hands to help them articulate thoughts and, often, to influence others. Politicians know this very well. Each time you see President George Bush or Vice President Dan Quayle giving a speech, you see a studied use of the hands that attempts to communicate leadership and security to the people watching. The hands also compensate for our inability to fully express ourselves with words. Hand gestures become more animated when we are frustrated (we throw up our hands in despair, for example) or angry. Hands are also used to distract us from what is being said—perhaps from the emptiness of the words or the importance of their meaning. A hand gesture can reinforce a statement; a person can slam a hand down on a table, or punch a fist into the palm of a hand. Or a speaker can soothe or distract us with more lifting gestures that seem to diminish the weight or energy of the words he or she is using.

We must recognize what a person is trying to do with his or her hands when talking to us. The hands are used subconsciously and consciously, and we must be alert to both.

In Oriental diagnosis, we see the hands in a far different way from, say, the way the student of anatomy sees them. The palm, metacarpus, thumb, and fingers all possess deep personal meaning. They reveal our inner beings in ways similar to the ways in which our faces reveal them. Let's have a closer look.

To begin with, the hands are a train-yard of acupuncture meridians. These meridians—six in all—flow down the arm and into the hand and fingers. The energy flows down the arms, through the hands and fingers, and out of the body. The fingers, therefore, are discharge points, or outlets for energy from the body. Very often, waste that cannot be eliminated in the normal ways—through the bowels, urine, breath, or skin—is channeled into the fingers, where it creates a variety of problems, including sores, ingrown nails, hangnails, infections, and arthritis.

Warts are very common on the fingers. In Oriental medicine, warts are seen as a discharge of excess animal protein and fats. When a wart appears on a particular finger, it means that animal protein and fats are being discharged from the corresponding part of the body.

Extend one of your arms forward so that the palm and inside of your arm are facing you. Three meridians flow along the inside of your arm and down into your fingers. At the upper ridge of the inside of your arm is the lung meridian. It flows through the middle of the great muscle at the base of the thumb, and then down into the thumb itself. Problems that appear on the thumb, therefore, may indicate trouble in the lungs.

Often you find the great muscle of the thumb turning blue or red. When it is blue, the lung on that side of the body is stagnant. Ki and blood are trapped in the lung, and there is little movement. Carbon dioxide is accumulating in the alveoli, the minute sacs in which blood interacts with oxygen.

A blue color in the thumb also indicates coolness, which further helps to stagnate the blood and energy in that meridian and in the lungs. A person with a blue thumb muscle may be depressed or feeling deep grief over the loss of a particular relationship.

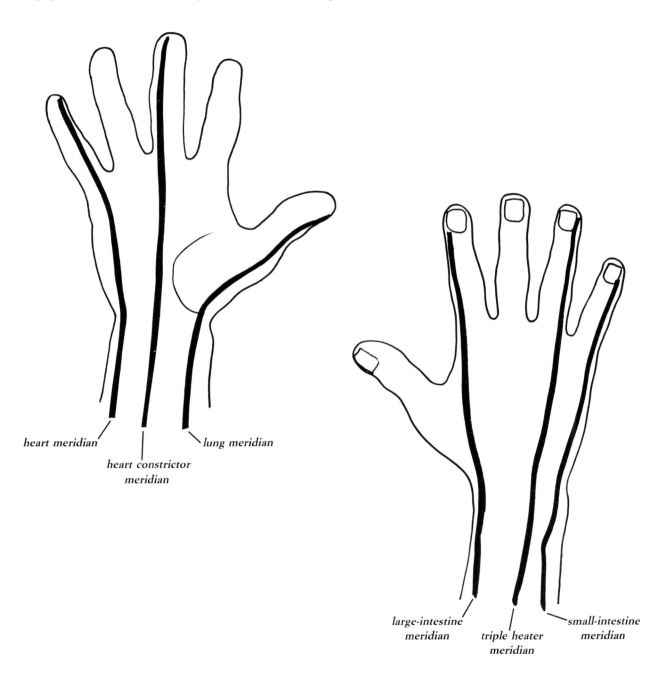

heart meridian

heart constrictor
meridian

lung meridian

large-intestine
meridian

triple heater
meridian

small-intestine
meridian

The lungs take in oxygen, provide it to the blood, and cleanse the blood of carbon dioxide. They then exhale the carbon dioxide into the air. In Oriental diagnosis, we see the lungs as the recipients of ki. We live in a world of energy that is all around us and within us. We breathe in drafts of this energy in the form of air and ki and make both available to our blood and cells.

When the lungs are troubled, our capacity to take in oxygen and ki is diminished. Therefore, life force—in the forms of both ki and oxygen—is weaker. We sense our weakened state. Meanwhile, problems seem to grow, making us depressed about the possible outcome of events. If we are depressed, we must strengthen our lungs and do more and deeper breathing.

When you see a blue color in the thumb I recommend that the person stop eating all dairy products, fatty foods, and especially sugar, including raw fruit and fruit juice. Sugar and fruit sugars injure the lungs and are one of the main causes of pneumonia. Ask the person gently whether he or she takes drugs, including pharmaceuticals. If the person takes recreational drugs, suggest that the lung problem is related to the drug use and urge the person, respectfully, to stop using all recreational drugs. The person should also eat plenty of leafy green vegetables, grated gingerroot on vegetables, and boiled or pressure-cooked brown rice. These foods help to reestablish good circulation and movement in the lungs.

The person should also do more active physical exercise, especially aerobic exercise, such as bicycle riding, running, jumping jacks, and brisk walking. This will cause deep breathing, removing stagnant carbon dioxide. It will also move blood and oxygen through the lungs rapidly and clear up congestion. Gradually, the emotional depression will clear up and the person will feel stronger and more vital again.

When the thumb or muscle is red, there is a concentration of what Oriental healers call fire energy in the lungs. The cause is too much emotion, too many spicy foods, and an ambition that is inappropriate in the person's current circumstances. We tend to want things to flow to us more rapidly than they do. When you see redness in the thumb, ask the person whether he or she has been emotionally upset of late or tends to be short-tempered. Ask if there has been frustration or more stress than usual.

Recommend the same diet as above, but also ask the person to avoid all spices, hot foods, peppers, and hard liquor. The person with a fiery condition in the lungs should walk and stroll more. He or she should relieve tension and anxiety by spending more time in nature. More relaxing activities are necessary, such as prayer, silent meditation, and listening to peaceful music by classical composers. People with fire energy in the lungs should learn to detach more from their lives and to appreciate the beauty that surrounds them and is within them. They should try not to identify themselves so thoroughly with their ambitions.

Sometimes there is redness or swelling along the cuticle or along the left and right edges of the nail. This indicates a discharge from the lungs caused by too much yin food or by drugs. A person with such redness or swelling should follow the same dietary advice above and avoid all sugar and pharmaceuticals.

Hangnails are a symptom of extremes in eating and in emotional states, such as too much passion, frustration, or anger. A person with a hangnail should try to bring balance to the diet and emotional life by following the advice above.

Occasionally you see lumps or skin eruptions on the thumb. If these bumps are white, they are caused by the elimination of dairy foods and animal fats from the lung that corresponds with that side of the body. If the skin eruptions are red, they are caused by excess sugar, fruit, fruit juice, spices, and, perhaps, some type of drug.

Finally, to bring more healing energy to the lungs, it is good to rub-down the great muscle at the base of the thumb, and also massage the thumb itself. In the center of the thumb muscle is the fire point on the lung meridian. If you are depressed, stimulate this deeply. It will bring more ki to the lungs and encourage blood circulation. If you have redness at the muscle, gently massage this point and picture the excess energy in your lungs dispersing and leaving your body. Take one thumb in your other hand and rotate it clockwise for a few minutes. Once you have done this, rotate it counterclockwise.

In the middle of the inside of the arm is the heart constrictor meridian, which controls the flow of energy and the circulation. This meridian flows down the middle of the hand to the tip of the middle finger.

There is a place on the inside of the arm, about two inches above the wrist lines at the base of the hand, which is an excellent point for stimulating the circulation. Press this point deeply and you will feel a certain electric sensation. You may also feel some pain. Do this massage on both arms.

The etymology of language always reveals some subtle psychological meanings. We sometimes use words and their associations without consciously knowing their subtler meanings. This is also true of our deeper and unconscious knowledge of our bodies. The middle finger has always been associated with sex; interestingly, the middle finger is the recipient of the sexual energy that flows through the heart constrictor meridian, down the middle of the arm, to the middle finger.

To strengthen ki energy to the sex organs and improve blood circulation, rotate the middle finger for several minutes, both clockwise and counterclockwise. Gently tug on the finger, using a quick pulling motion and then letting go. This will release pent-up energy in the meridian and help promote the circulation and sexual energy.

At the bottom of the arm, on the inside, is the heart meridian, which flows to the little finger. It flows along the bottom of the little finger and, at the last joint, turns upward to the top of the finger and terminates right at the inside of the nail.

When there is redness along the cuticle of the little finger or at the edges of the nail, the body is discharging excess energy from the heart area. Check the tips of your fingers, especially the little one. If the tips are red, the body is attempting to eliminate excess energy from the fingers. If the little finger's tip is red, the heart is overstimulated. This usually stems from the consumption of too many stimulants, especially caffeine or spicy foods.

A person with heart disease may complain of stiffness or numbness in the little finger, indicating the danger of heart attack or stroke. There is an important heart meridian point on the inside of the little finger at the nail. Press this point deeply to stimulate the heart meridian, especially if there is some type of heart condition, such as angina pectoris or atherosclerosis. By massaging this point on both hands, you stimulate your heart with ki. (This manipulation can help to establish better health, though it is not a substitute for a healthier diet and a sound life-style.)

Now turn your hand over so that the back faces you. On the outside of the arm are three more meridians: the large intestine, triple heater, and small intestine.

The large-intestine meridian runs from the index finger, up the crook of the arm, over the top of the shoulder, along the sides of the mouth, to a point where the nostril meets the face. On the hand, the meridian flows across the back of the hands, over the protruding muscle between the thumb and index finger.

Acupuncture points are generally called *tsubos*, and there is an important tsubo directly in the center of the large muscle between the thumb and index finger on the back of the hand. It is called Go Ko Ku. Massage this point by pressing the tip of your thumb into the muscle, searching for the "hot spot," where there is the greatest sensitivity. When you have located this point, you will feel a sort of electric sensation and, depending on the health of your intestines, perhaps a degree of pain. A sharp pain indicates some trapped energy in the large intestine. There may be stagnation and constipation. However, those who suffer from diarrhea may also feel considerable pain when pressing this point. Press the point deeply in a clockwise direction. This will tone and help reestablish harmony in the meridian and large intestine.

Sometimes this point will be very sensitive on one hand and not sensitive at all on the other. This means that the painful side has much

Press the point between your index finger and thumb. A hard and tight feeling may indicate intestinal problems.

stagnant ki, while the insensitive side is deficient of energy. Massage both sides equally to bring a balanced condition to the large intestine meridian.

Massaging this point is also good for bringing on a bowel movement. Go Ko Ku is almost miraculous at stimulating the large intestine and helping it eliminate waste. Go Ko Ku also brings a certain balance and harmony to the overall system. Whenever you are feeling ill or weak, sit down in a quiet place and press Go Ko Ku. It will bring a degree of stability to your whole system. I also press this point when I receive dental work, in order to feel less pain.

It is very important always to massage the same points on both sides of the body. We are striving to create balance; therefore, we stimulate or relax both sides of the body equally.

Down the middle of the outside of your arm flows the triple heater meridian. As I mentioned in chapter 3, the triple heater meridian controls the energy in the three main parts of the thorax—the upper part being the heart and lungs; the middle part being the stomach, spleen, and pancreas; and the lower part corresponding to the intestines and sex organs.

The triple heater meridian flows along the back of the hand and into the ring finger. It is associated with the heart and the overall unity of the body, mind, and spirit; I believe that is why we wear our wedding rings on this finger.

Occasionally you see older people whose heads shake up and down as they talk. There can be several causes for this shaking, including Parkinson's disease. One other cause is an imbalance in the triple heater meridian. The three energy centers are uncoordinated. One—perhaps the heart center—is overstimulated; there is too much energy here. One or both of the other centers—usually the intestines—are weaker. The excess heart energy causes the nervous system to become overstimulated, leading to this shaking of the head.

Recommended remedies are exercise, Ohashiatsu, and a change to a more balanced diet that enhances the condition of the intestines and diminishes the energy around the heart.

To bring more balanced energy to the triple heater, stimulate the ring finger in the same way as mentioned above: both clockwise and counterclockwise, tugging gently on the finger and then releasing it.

Finally, two meridians are located in the little finger: the heart, described above, and the small intestine.

The small-intestine meridian runs from the nail of the little finger, up the back of the arm, to the shoulder blade, up the back of the neck, to a point just in front of the ear hole on the side of the face. Skin eruptions here may suggest congestion and stagnation in the small-intestine meridian.

Occasionally the pad or muscle at the edge of the hand below the little finger is excessively red. This means that there is blood stagnation in the small intestine and heart meridians. The person with such redness likely has trouble adequately nourishing himself or herself in life. In terms of digestion, such a red color means that assimilation of nutrients is hampered. Check the bottom lip. Is it too tight or swollen? If it is tight, it indicates that the small intestine is overly contracted. Blood is trapped and circulation is limited. The person needs to do more exercises that stretch the midsection and bring increased circulation to the small intestine. The diet should be more yin—that is, lighter, wetter, with fewer baked goods. This person should avoid all red meat, fatty foods, and excessive amounts of oil until the condition improves.

If the bottom lip is swollen, it means that the small intestine is expanded and weak. Depending on the person's overall health, he or she can eat more grains and foods that are cooked longer, such as beans.

A wonderful exercise for the hands is to shake them vigorously for a few minutes. This increases ki along the meridians in the hands and improves circulation.

Let's look at the relationship between the fingers and the palm.

If the palm is longer than the fingers, it indicates that the person works more practically and less intellectually. This is especially true if the palm is big and square and the fingers are short and wide. Short, wide fingers indicate an ability as a builder, carpenter, or mechanic. The person with such fingers understands how things work.

Square hands indicate a lack of interest in intellectual matters and a preference for basic, simple pleasures. A person with such hands enjoys straight talk and is direct and even blunt; he or she has a no-frills approach to life. Such people are more physical than mental. They are lovers of hearty foods and will eat indiscriminately. I advise them to guard against abusing their hearts and circulatory systems, especially with fatty and oily foods and meat.

People whose fingers are longer than their palms are highly intellectual and have distinct mental abilities. They tend to be more gentle, passive, and artistic. They are discriminating in their tastes, especially in the kinds of activities they enjoy (they lean toward the arts) and the types of food they will eat. I noticed that they can be picky eaters, but especially enjoy sweets and wine.

People whose palms and fingers are equal in length tend to have more balanced natures—that is, they can enjoy both physical and mental pursuits. Their balanced natures invariably lead them to white-collar jobs, or to positions of leadership in labor-intensive work.

In general, the squarer the hand, the stronger the constitution. The pointier and narrower the hand, the more delicate the constitution.

The hands indicate how flexible our minds and bodies are. Let's do an exercise to see how flexible our hands are. Place your hands together in a prayer position in front of your chest. Now raise your palms upward and outward, while keeping the fingers of both hands touching each other. You should be able to create two right angles with your fingers and the backs of your hands. In other words, your palms should be horizontal while your fingers are vertical, all the while keeping the fingers of both hands touching.

If you can do this exercise, you have reasonably good flexibility of hands, mind, and body.

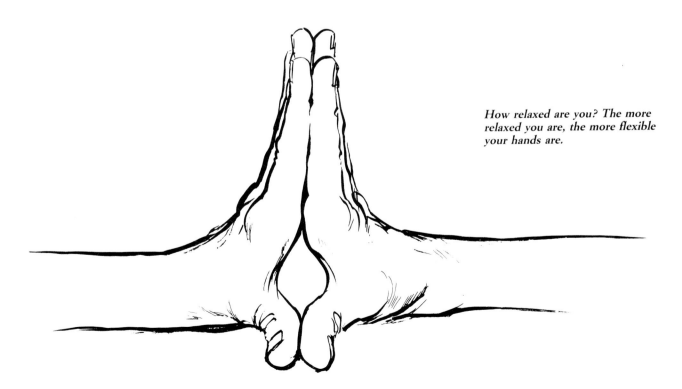

How relaxed are you? The more relaxed you are, the more flexible your hands are.

Triangle nail: yin constitution.

Hands that are supple and flexible indicate a person who is open to a variety of opinions and has a flexible intellect. Usually such people are creative and find it easy to go around obstacles in their path. Their relationships are less conflicted and tense.

Hands that are inflexible or tight indicate a conceptual person, perhaps rigid and even stubborn. If the hands are inflexible and strong, the person does not mind meeting obstacles head on and will fight to assert his or her principles. People with strong, inflexible hands tend to be confrontational when they deem it necessary, which may be more often than not.

Vertical lines on the nail: liver problem.

Spoon nail: anemia, low blood pressure.

Round nail: yang constitution.

Round nail: lung and breathing problem.

Square nail: high blood pressure, strong constitution.

Press the nail and see how quickly the red color returns. The faster it returns, the better your circulation.

Bump on the nail: worms in your intestine.

Groove on the nail: malnutrition, poor digestion.

1

The Feet

As I mentioned in chapter 1, part of your success as a practitioner of Oriental diagnosis depends on your ability to examine people without making them feel uncomfortable. You must make a person feel relaxed if he or she is to reveal himself or herself to you. Sometimes people make a great show of facial expressions or hand gestures, trying consciously to distract you from seeing deeply into their inner nature. This is understandable and entirely human: no one likes to have his or her private life examined. As long as your intentions are honorable and you are committed to being of assistance, you have a good chance of helping your friend relax. When you are having trouble diagnosing, however, look carefully at the feet. Often you will see much more than you think.

I remember very well seeing former Philippine president Ferdinand Marcos on television when he was being ousted from power some years ago. Just before he was forced to leave the country, he gave numerous speeches in which he tried to communicate power and control over his country's crisis. I saw one of those speeches, during which the television camera showed his whole body. He was seated at a table with a microphone in front of him. His hair was slicked back, his face a mask of indifference, power, and control. His white shirt was well starched. As he spoke, his hands and face communicated artificial strength, but his feet revealed his true condition.

His pants were high on his calf, revealing his socks, both of which drooped in an unkempt way. It looked to me as if his socks did not match the rest of his outfit, but in any case they were utterly incongruous with it; while everything about him was starched and controlled, his socks were rolled down low, near the tops of his shoes. They made him look like a scared little boy. Also, Marcos's feet were not planted firmly on the floor, but moved back and forth and drummed nervously beneath the table. His feet revealed his true condition: the foundation of his life was crumbling.

Many millions of Americans today have foot problems. Among the most common problems are bunions, calluses, and swollen areas that prevent people from standing or walking comfortably. Many people rationalize these bumps and bunions by blaming them on their shoes—"My shoe rubs me there"—or perhaps their clumsiness—"I must have bumped my foot without realizing it." Your shoe may very well rub you at that point now—indeed, it must, since the bump sticks out so far—but what caused the bump to come out in the first place? You've been walking on the same feet your whole life. Why didn't the bump appear sooner? Why do children rarely have such bumps and bunions? Even more mystifying is the question of why these growths occur where they do. Why a bump on the fourth toe, for example, or on the side of the foot, just above the big toe?

Actually, the original cause was not your shoes, though they may be a problem now, too. The real cause is far deeper and more revealing of your life.

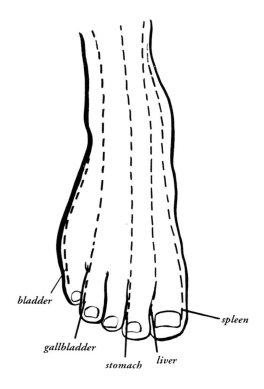

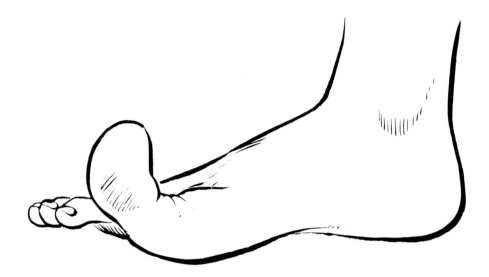

Big toe is large, points up, and is occasionally swollen: big eater, violent, easily upset.

Let's examine the feet more closely and unveil some of their mysteries.

Like the hand, the foot is a train-yard of meridian lines. Six meridians flow up and down your legs and through various parts of your feet. There is a type of foot massage known as foot reflexology. The theory behind foot reflexology is that by massaging certain points on the foot, you actually stimulate, tone or balance, or sedate all the organs and regions of the body. I encourage people to walk barefoot even for short periods each day to improve circulation in the feet and stimulate other parts of the body. By walking barefoot, we stimulate and energize our health. (I'll discuss foot reflexology shortly.)

The big toe contains two meridians, the liver and the spleen. The liver meridian begins at the top of the big toe, where the nail meets the cuticle, and runs up the inside of the leg, along the calf and thigh, to the groin. From there it moves across the side of the stomach region to a point at the side of the rib cage, and then up to a point just below the nipple. (Remember that each meridian is one of a pair. Each foot has a liver meridian that runs in mirror image along the corresponding side of the body.) There is a point on the top of the foot near the place where the tendons of the big toe and second toe converge. You can find this point easily by following these two tendons with your finger up from the toes to the place where the tendons meet. The point is in the soft tissue right before the two tendons come together. Probe this point; it is usually very sensitive. By pressing deeply here with your thumb, you can stimulate ki energy in the liver meridian.

The spleen meridian runs from the outside of the big toe, along the inside of the foot, up the inside of the shin, across the knee and thigh, to the groin area, up the side of the stomach to the armpit, and then hooks below the armpit to a point on the back.

Many people have a large bunion on the side of the foot right above the big toe. This bunion, sometimes red or inflamed, appears as a bony mass. It indicates a sluggish, tired spleen from too many sweet foods and inadequate amounts of minerals. People with this condition tend to suffer from arthritis.

This bunion appears because the spleen is attempting to eliminate excess energy and waste along the spleen meridian. The energy is blocked at the spleen and tends to back up along the meridian, causing swelling of capillaries and, eventually, a bony mass on the side of the foot. At this point, the shoe begins to rub against the swollen area. If the person continues to treat the spleen badly, excesses will continue to accumulate, calcify, and create a large bunion.

In Oriental diagnosis, we say that such a bunion suggests a very stubborn person.

As I explained in chapter 3, the stomach meridian runs down from the face, along the front of the body, and down the outside of the calf, and terminates in the second toe. For this reason, I regard the second toe as indicative of the condition of a person's eating and digestive tract.

Again, swelling of the second toe indicates that the organ itself is burdened and is attempting to eliminate excess energy trapped both in the organ and along the meridian.

A longer second toe indicates a very powerful stomach and stomach meridian. The person with a longer second toe will have a strong appetite, will tend to overeat, easily becoming overweight, and may suffer from gout or arthritis in the end.

People with strong stomachs tend to believe they can eat anything without regret. "I have an iron stomach," they like to say. They do not realize that they do not have an iron liver. Consequently, they put things in their stomachs that their livers cannot deal with. Oriental healers say that such people are living according to their strengths, not their weaknesses. In this case, they are being destroyed by their strength. If a particular organ were weaker, they would have to moderate their behavior because the organ would give them symptoms and discomfort, but the organ remains silent and other less strong organs suffer and rapidly degenerate.

If a person abuses his or her liver consistently, the person will grow angrier and more hostile, suffering from explosions of emotion over which he or she has little control.

Such a person should reduce consumption of gourmet and rich food and drink, especially meat and fat and hard liquor.

In general, a toe that overlaps another indicates that the organ in-

Second toe is longer than the other toes: great appetite.

dicated by the overlapping toe is stronger than the organ represented by the overlapped toe.

If the big toe overlaps the second toe, it means the stomach meridian is weaker compared to the liver. A person with an overlapping big toe must avoid stimulants, refined sugars, and acidic foods, which harm the stomach. Such a person probably suffers from stomach problems and consequently is prudent about what he or she eats. These people must be very careful to chew food well and avoid food and drink that overstimulate the liver, such as alcohol, excessively sour foods, and strong spices. This kind of food and drink will further complicate the already troubled condition. In this case, the liver energy should be subdued, while the stomach energy is made stronger. (See dietary advice and exercises in chapter 9.)

The gallbladder meridian runs down the outside of the leg, across the top of the foot, to the top of the fourth toe. This toe, by the way, is often the site of a large bunion. In Oriental diagnosis, we say that when a bunion appears on the fourth toe, the gallbladder is troubled. The person likely eats too many fatty and oily foods, causing the liver and gallbladder to become congested with cholesterol. A large brown bunion on the fourth toe may reveal a tendency toward gallstones, and a fiery temper. A person with such a bunion may suffer from explosions of emotion—anger can flare up suddenly and then just as suddenly evaporate.

The bladder meridian runs down the back, over the buttocks, and down the back of the leg to the heel. Actually, the bladder meridian divides into parallel highways down the back. The highways join at the back of the knee. From there it runs down the calf, along the outside of the foot to the little toe. Well-developed and flexible little toes indicate that a person is less likely to have lower-back trouble. A pregnant woman with flexible little toes will probably not have a difficult time with delivery.

The kidney meridian begins at a point at the bottom of the foot, in the center. This point, kidney 1, is called "bubbling spring" or "gushing spring." If this area is healthy, well developed, thick, soft, and warm, the person may have a long life with good health. If you probe this point, you will sense a deep well of energy. Massaging this point helps to strengthen the kidneys which, as mentioned in chapter 2, are the source of the fundamental energy of the body and spirit. The meridian continues along the arch, makes a loop at the heel, and runs up the side of the leg, up the center of the body, to the inside of the clavicle.

Earlier I mentioned foot reflexology, the philosophy that the organs of the body can be stimulated by massaging certain points in the feet.

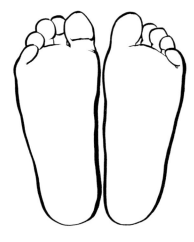

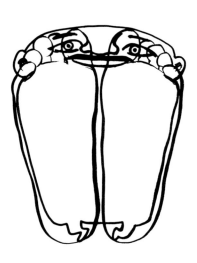

The micro represents the macro: if you project the body onto the feet, you will see their relationship.

Once again, this exemplifies the rule that in Oriental diagnosis the macro can be seen in the micro, and the micro in the macro. The foot is a constellation of points that relate to the entire body.

Foot reflexology concentrates mainly on the bottom, or underside, of the feet. We can draw a map on the bottom of the foot that shows the various points and their corresponding organs. The accompanying chart illustrates these points.

In general, the foot reflexology points in many cases correspond to the particular meridians mentioned above. At the bottom of the big toe, in the eleven o'clock position, is a spleen point. Massaging here provides ki to the spleen. Beneath the second and third toes, where the toes join the foot, are points that correspond with the heart and spleen, respectively. At the same place on the fourth toe is a point that corresponds to the lungs. On the bottom of the foot at the base of the small toe is a point that corresponds to the kidneys. If you massage these points, you will find that they are noticeably more sensitive than other parts of the body.

The ball and pad of the foot correspond to the shoulders and lungs. Directly in the center of the foot, just below the pad, is "bubbling spring," the kidney point.

Along the arch are three general areas that correspond to the nose, throat, and chest. On the other side of the foot, along the edge, is a large area that corresponds to the upper abdomen and waist.

In general, the heel corresponds to the kidneys, by virtue of the fact that the bladder and kidney meridians flow through the heel area. But the bottom of the foot at the heel also corresponds with the lower abdomen. The lowest point on the heel, at the six o'clock position, is a point for the rectum, and the eight o'clock position is a point that corresponds to the uterus.

Massage each point vigorously to stimulate and help improve the condition of these organs.

Everyone loves a foot massage, especially when it is gentle, firm, and caring. Many people have very sensitive and ticklish feet, so touching feet must be approached very gently. It is good to start by rubbing the feet, rather than immediately probing for the variolus points. Rubbing the feet causes improved circulation and relaxes the foot. You must massage both feet; don't neglect either one. Otherwise, you will create left-right imbalances in the body.

Once you have rubbed the foot adequately, begin massaging the Achilles tendon. You are massaging the kidney and bladder meridians, which will stimulate the reproductive functions as well. Massage firmly and deeply. Do not use a jerking motion. Be slow and gentle, making sure to probe the tendon and heel area. Visualize the breaking up of stagnant energy in the kidney, bladder, and sex organs.

When you have finished, place the foot firmly on the floor and begin

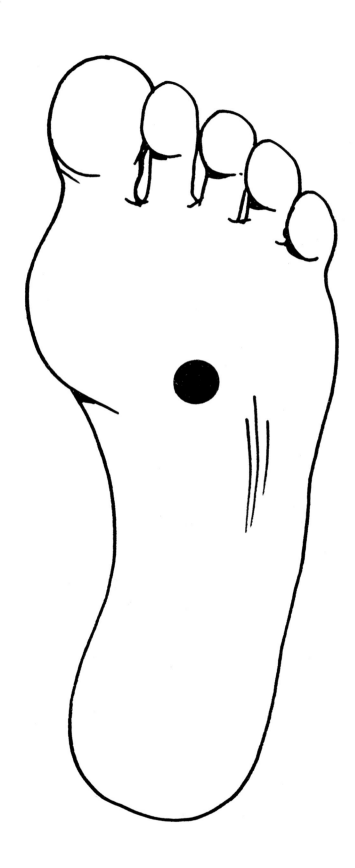

The number-one point of the kidney meridian: yu sen, *or "bubbling spring." For general fatigue.*

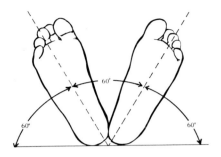

Normal position: the ideal condition of the feet; the hip sockets are balanced, as are the legs and the shoulders.

to massage the top of the foot—the metacarpal—from a place just above where the leg joins the foot, downward toward the first two toes. Massage deeply and firmly. Find the liver point where the tendons of the first two toes join. With your thumb, press deeply here. There will likely be a sharp, electric pain. Do not overstimulate this point, but massage it deeply while imagining stagnant energy in the liver breaking up and being released.

Turn your foot over and pull and bend the toes on each foot. Pull the toes all at once and then each toe individually. Slightly rotate the toes. This will stimulate ki to the various organs and will allow excess energy to escape from the terminal meridian points.

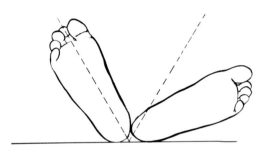

The left foot is turned out more than 60 degrees—in this example, 90 degrees. This indicates that the left hip socket is loose. The left leg is shorter, and more weight is put on the left foot.

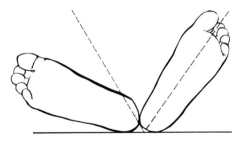

The right leg is turned out more than 60 degrees. This indicates that the right hip socket is loose. The right leg is shorter, and more weight is put on the right foot.

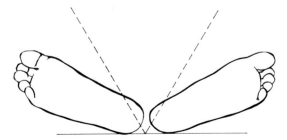

When both feet are turned out more than 60 degrees, as in this case, both hip sockets are loose.

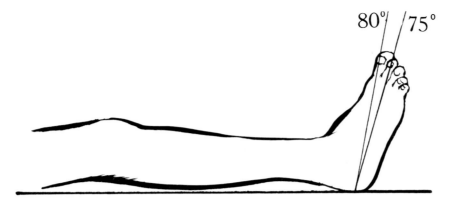

Seventy-five to 80 degrees is ideal.

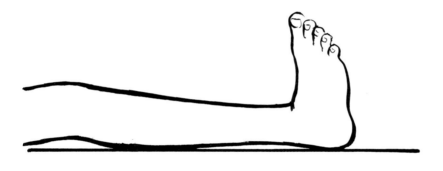

More than 90 degrees: stomach meridian is jitsu, too tight.

Ninety degrees: good appetite, strong health, but restless.

Less than 60 degrees: a weak constitution, poor health, chronic sickness.

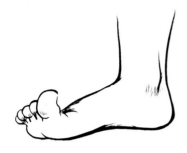

Toes are bent up: active, aggressive, and easily upset.

Now gently pound the bottom of your feet with a loosely closed fist. Remember to pound both feet. When you have finished pounding the entire bottom of the foot, deeply massage "bubbling spring," or the number-one point of the kidney meridian, with your thumb. Massage the other points that I discussed earlier. Do this to both feet.

Vigorously massaging both feet, every day, will have great impact on your health. You will stimulate all the organs of your body and release much pent-up energy that is causing foot problems.

Your feet are the foundation of your body. No one is happy if his or her feet hurt. You stand on your feet. Give them the attention they deserve.

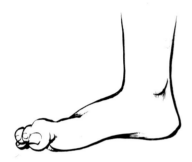

Toes are bent down ("hammer toes"): tense and nervous.

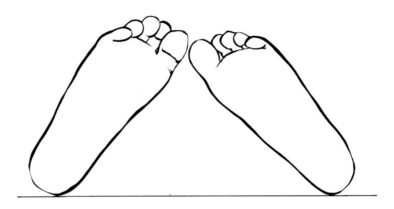

Both feet are turned inward: both hip sockets are tight; spleen, liver, and kidney meridians are jitsu.

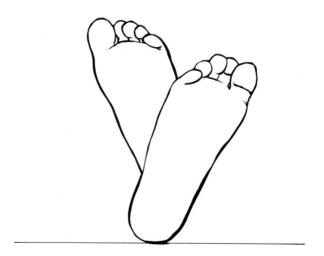

Right foot is on the left foot (right leg is longer than the left leg): breathing, chest, sinus problems.

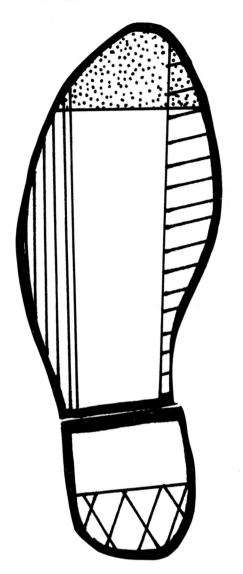

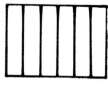

outside

inside

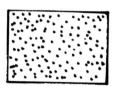

toetip

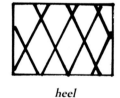

heel

Shoe diagnosis: the area where the shoe is worn out is where we put more of our weight.

THE STORIES SHOES TELL

Now that you know about the feet and meridians, you can begin to see the importance of many of the "smaller" details and characteristics of the body. Even a person's shoes can tell you the story of that person's life.

I like to tell a story about the owner of a Japanese country inn, or *ryokan*. This particular owner was very wise. He secretly possessed a very high understanding of Oriental diagnosis. Just as it is the custom in Japan to take off your shoes when you enter a house, people also take off their shoes when they enter a ryokan. The wise man who ran this particular ryokan could determine the characters of his customers

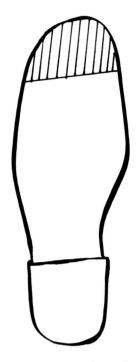

Toetip is worn out: always in a hurry, neurotic.

Heel is worn out: kidney problems, lower-back ache.

by examining their shoes, and thereby decided in which room to place each customer. He could tell, for example, whether a particular customer snored, in which case the customer would be placed in a room far enough away from the other guests so as not to disturb their sleep. The inn owner could also tell whether a customer should be near the bathroom, and whether or not he should pay in advance. Judging by the quality of the customer's shoes, the owner could tell also how much the customer could afford to pay. In this way, the wise owner could be generous to those who he felt needed generosity, and charge those full price who could afford the best.

As a longtime student of Oriental diagnosis, I, too, am constantly observing the shoes for clues to character, health, and a person's direction in life. The bottom of the shoe is the most hidden, of course. But remember, the most hidden parts of us are also the most revealing.

The shoes are interesting because they are the least attended to of our clothing, yet require the most personal attention, or maintenance. Many of you could not tolerate dirty shirts or a soiled suit, but you usually can "stand" dirty shoes. A person with well-cared-for shoes is a person who attends to the little details of his or her life. Another interesting fact about shoes is that they directly reflect a person's means. We almost never spend more than we can afford on shoes. A person of modest means is more likely to buy an expensive suit or dress or tie than an expensive pair of shoes. If the shoes are very expensive, it usually reveals a person of means.

To diagnose a person by examining the bottoms of his or her shoes, we must see where the wear is unbalanced—that is, where the shoes are excessively worn. Each of us puts more weight on one part of our foot than another. In Japan there is a set of scales that can determine which part of the foot a person places more weight on—the front, the heel, the inside, or the outside. These scales are attached to a computer, which can analyze the character of the person according to which part of the foot he places most of his or her weight on.

Just by looking at a pair of shoes, you can tell much about a person's overall structural distortions: where he or she places the weight of his body; whether he or she has a wide or narrow foot or is overweight or light-footed.

In my classes, I entertain my students by picking up a couple of pairs of shoes at random and, without knowing whom the shoes belong to, beginning to analyze their owners' characters. For example, if the front part of a shoe, near the first two toes, is more worn than the rest, I know that the owner's stomach meridian is very active. This means that the person is always hungry. He or she is therefore impatient and nervous about the outcome of events—fearing that desire, or appetite, will not be satisfied. Such people have good appetites and are hungry for life, but their impatience makes them prone to accidents. "The person who owns this shoe bumps his head a lot," I may say.

If the back of the shoe is excessively worn, it means that the owner's kidneys are overworked. The person likely consumes too much liquid and may suffer from lower-back ache. He or she may be sluggish, easily fatigued, and fearful—hesitant about the future and fearful of opportunity. This person is searching for security, but likely cannot find it. Naturally, this person is not an adventurous one.

The area near the arch reveals the condition of the spleen and liver; both these meridians, you will recall, run through the inner part of the foot. If this part of the shoe is worn, it means the person is probably knock-kneed, and places excessive weight on the inside of the foot at the arch. The liver and spleen are overtaxed. The person is likely somewhat antisocial, timid, and perhaps frustrated, especially sexually. The reproductive organs are probably troubled, complicating relationships with the opposite sex. The person may suffer a marked degree of confusion when confronted with important decisions. He or she likely has neck and shoulder pain, because of the imbalance in the body weight and posture.

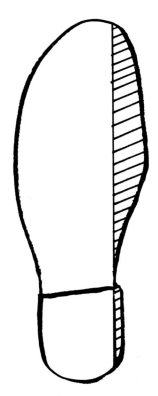

Inside is worn out: problems with intestines, sex organs.

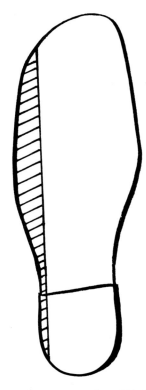

Outside is worn out: gallbladder, liver problems.

You can control your face to some degree (some people do it better than others), but it is hard to control your toes, or the way you place the weight of your body on your feet. Therefore, these characteristics are much more true and revealing about who you really are.

When the outside part of the shoe is excessively worn, it means that the person is somewhat bow-legged and places most of his or her weight on the outer part of the foot, along the bladder and gallbladder meridians. This is a person who likes spicy, sensual foods, but is an indiscriminate eater. This person is probably overweight, and suffers from anger, fear, and hostility. He or she may have difficulty making decisions and probably has a practical nature. This person probably suffers from shoulder pain, due to the imbalance in the body caused by the uneven distribution of weight.

Sometimes you see that the big toe area of the shoe is more worn than the rest. This means that the owner's liver energy is excessive, or jitsu. As I mentioned in chapter 3, such a person is driven, goal-oriented, and a workaholic. Anger is never far from the surface, but this person is probably trying to control it.

When the shoes are clean, it reveals a meticulous person, one who cares much about details. When the shoes are moderately well cared for, it means the person is more relaxed about his or her image. Such people may be more concerned with the substance of their personalities or the quality of their work. If the shoes are particularly dirty or ill-kept, the person probably suffers from a high degree of chaos in his or her life—the result of some physical or mental illness, or perhaps financial difficulty.

The smell of a person's shoes reflects his or her diet. If the shoes give off a strong, repugnant, sour smell, the person likely eats too many animal foods, including dairy products; sweats too much, indicating overworked kidneys; and probably suffers from being overweight and high blood pressure. If the shoes smell sweet, the person consumes too many sweets and may suffer from some problem related to the spleen and pancreas, such as hyperglycemia or diabetes. A salty smell indicates that the kidneys are overworked; a pungent smell indicates some imbalance in the large intestine.

You can tell much about a person's occupation from his or her shoes. If the right heel is more worn than the left, the person probably spends a lot of time driving a car. The wear comes from keeping the right foot on the gas pedal. A person who stands for many hours will have shoes that bulge or stretch on the sides, because the weight of the body makes the foot widen and flatten out.

I have a special feeling about shoes because I got my first pair when I was seven years old. The war had left my family, and so many others, somewhat poor, and it was a long time before my parents could afford to purchase shoes for me. Finally, when I was seven, I got my first pair.

When I first got them, I was so happy and so in love with those shoes that I slept with them. I couldn't wait to get up in the morning and wear my shoes to school. When I finally got to school, however, I saw that not so many kids were wearing shoes. Suddenly I was self-conscious and miserable, so I took off my shoes and hid them in my backpack. I was ashamed that I had something my friends did not.

The shoes are no different from any other part of the body. The micro reflects the macro—meaning that in the smallest part of the body, the clues to the whole nature are revealed.

It is not so important *what* you are reading when you examine the shoes—or any part of the body, for that matter. The most important point is *why* you are reading.

People are always asking, "How can I be happy and healthy?" or "How can I be enlightened? Should I go to India or Japan?" I tell them, "Look at your shoes. You are standing on your answer." The secrets of your life are written on your body; they are being worn into the soles of your shoes. Just read them. The universe is seeking to give us the answers we need. The information is flowing to us constantly from many directions, in many forms. We block that information by failing to live in harmony with it. We have many imbalances. These imbalances act like rocks in the river of life: they get in the way of the information that flows to us. Remove the rocks and the answers will come as if out of the blue. Actually, the answers to our most important questions come from within us. All we have to do is learn to see; to read the body; to listen to the answers; and to follow the guidance provided us by the universe itself.

The Skin and Hair

THE SKIN, WHICH IS THE BODY'S LARGEST organ, is responsible for a range of functions, including the regulation of the body's temperature (by perspiration); the inhalation of oxygen and exhalation of carbon dioxide; the sensing of the physical world through touch; and the elimination of toxins through the pores. Below the surface, the skin holds the hair follicles, and contains sweat glands and sebaceous glands, which hold fat.

We all know that the skin is a very sensitive organ and responds immediately to changes in our external environment. Anyone who has experienced embarrassment knows the flaring heat and redness of a blush. The skin undergoes many other changes. Sometimes our skin appears pale, other times red, or yellow, or even gray or brown. Freckles emerge and, for many, disappear again. Sometimes our skin is wetter than normal; the palms of our hands, for example, are sometimes exceedingly wet. At other times they may be dry.

Occasionally our skin becomes oily. Many people suffer from chronically oily skin. Various parts of our skin, including specific parts of the face, can be oilier than others—the nose can be oilier than the neck, for example. At times, the skin can be flaky and dry; at other times it can suffer from various eruptions, such as sores, rashes, and acne. All of this demonstrates that the skin is a highly sensitive, highly volatile organ that changes dramatically.

These changes inspire a variety of reactions from people. Some of us see the skin as our enemy. It simply does not behave as we would like it to. We say things like, "I have sensitive skin," or "I have oily skin," or "I have dry skin," as if such conditions were a permanent part of our makeup. It is true that genes play an important role in the texture, strength, and sensitivity of our skin, but it is equally true that no matter what our genetic makeup is, every one of us can have healthy, attractive skin. All we have to do is listen to the communications our skin sends us.

The skin is a marvelous organ because it reacts quickly and dramatically to our internal condition. Because of the skin's sensitivity, it can be used as a barometer for our lives, and we can read it. The skin can tell us, for example, whether or not our food is healthful; whether or not our environment is healthful; and whether or not our attitudes toward life are healthy. Stress, for example, can affect the skin. Hives— an itchy, swollen rash—is often associated with stress, or, more accurately, how we deal with stress.

Many of us regard sensitive skin as a curse, but in fact it is a blessing. Sensitive skin can be very beautiful, but only if you live in harmony with the external environment. You must eat the foods that suit your health and the health of your skin. If you do not, your appearance will be affected. In this way, the universe uses our vanity to guide us toward good health. If we behave properly—that is, if we take care of our health—our skin will be radiant, supple, bright, and shining, no matter how sensitive it may be. I consider that those who can eat all sorts of unhealthful foods and still look good are the ones that are in trouble, because their barometer cannot be used to guide them toward better health.

Let's look at all of these skin changes, one by one. I'll start with color. Before I begin, it's important to note that when I say white, yellow, or brown skin, I do not mean racial skin colors, but changes of skin color within each racial group. No one on the planet is truly white-skinned, of course. But within the Caucasian grouping, there are people whose skin color is more white than that of others. It is the same with Asians, Africans, Hispanics, Native Americans, Mediterraneans, and everyone else. Once again, we must look at each person individually to determine whether the skin appears healthy or shows a variation of the usual color, indicating some internal change.

THE COLORS OF THE SKIN

Since most people cover up the vast majority of their skin, I'll confine my discussion to facial color. If there are pigment changes elsewhere, check the meridian (see chapter 3) that flows through that area of the body. Generally, however, the explanations for each color given below will correspond to other parts of the body as well. For example, the color red generally relates to the heart and indicates an excess of yin influences in a person's life. If there is excessive redness on, say, the spleen meridian, it can mean consumption of too many yin substances—such as sugar, fruit, juices, and alcohol—and a deficiency of minerals.

RED

The color red, especially in the face, relates directly to the heart and circulatory system. Red skin is caused by the dilation of capillaries. Blood is rushing to the area, causing the surface of the skin to change to the color of blood. Anything that causes the heart to pump faster—such as sudden fright, embarrassment, laughter, or exercise—increases circulation and can cause the skin to redden. Generally, more yin foods cause the skin to become chronically red, because yin causes the peripheral capillaries to expand. Therefore, sweets, alcohol, many spices, highly emotional experiences (crying, screaming, laughing), and sudden embarrassments are generally more yin, and therefore have a greater effect on the peripheral circulation.

Yang things can quicken the heartbeat and circulation, of course. Exercise is a good example. Exercise is yang, in that it causes muscles to contract and the heart to beat faster. So when you see a red face, you must question what the cause is—yin or yang. Generally, if the cause is yang, the redness will go away as soon as the person cools off and circulation returns to normal. If the cause is yin, the redness will be chronic and will likely relate to the consumption of sweets, fruit, fruit juices, spices, and alcohol.

WHITE

White or very pale skin relates directly to the lungs and large intestine. When the lungs are congested or too tight, circulation is hampered and the skin turns white. When a person suffers from shock, chronic lung disease, or poor circulation, his or her skin turns white. All of these symptoms point to a lung and bronchial problem. Lungs are especially sensitive to cigarette smoking and to excess consumption of fat. Excess fat and cholesterol in the diet reduces the oxygen-carrying capacity of the blood. White skin also indicates deficient quantities of hemoglobin, the protein that carries oxygen and iron in the blood.

When there are intestinal disorders, including chronic constipation, blood becomes stagnant in the intestinal tract. This lack of circulation in the intestines causes poor blood flow to other parts of the body, including the lungs, and can be the cause of white or pale skin.

YELLOW

Yellow skin relates to the liver and gallbladder. Bile and other liver secretions cause the skin and eyes to become yellow. Jaundice, of course, is the best example of a liver disorder causing yellow skin.

BROWN

Generally, brown color relates to the kidneys. When the kidneys do not function optimally, the color of the blood will darken. This darkness will be passed on to the skin, especially to the area below the eyes and to the upper part of the cheeks. Brown around the bridge of the nose indicates a problem with the middle organs, especially the stomach, spleen, and pancreas, and excess consumption of yin foods.

BLUE

The color blue relates to the liver and stomach, spleen, and pancreas. Blue is often seen at the temples, on the bridge of the nose, and in the skin between the eyes. These areas correspond to the spleen and liver. A blue tinge indicates that both sets of organs are suffering from poor circulation. Consequently, they are excessively cool and stagnant. More yang influences, including more exercise, Ohashiatsu, and a general increase in physical activity, are necessary.

BEAUTY MARKS

Often you see dark moles or beauty marks on the face or other parts of the body. These marks are sometimes present at birth, but often appear later in life as well. I consider that such beauty marks are actually toxins discharged from the body. They sometimes appear along meridians. These marks are caused by the burning of excess carbohydrates, fats, and proteins. Check the meridian line where the beauty mark is found to tell which activity has been affected. In general, this meridian will be a little weaker than the others and should be treated accordingly.

OILY SKIN

Healthy skin should have a very slight oily sheen. Skin metabolizes vitamin D by combining sunlight and fat (oil is actually fat in liquid form). Since vitamin D is essential to health, a slight amount of oil on the skin is a sign of healthy metabolism. Most of us do not worry about a small amount of oil on the skin, however. We worry about too much oil.

The cause of excess oil on the skin is an excess of oils, fats, and animal foods in the diet. "Excess" is a relative word. If you suffer from oily skin, you are getting more oily and fatty food than you need for your constitution and current condition.

Oily skin also suggests a weak liver, gallbladder, heart, or pancreas.

The liver and gallbladder process fat and oils by providing bile acids. When the liver is congested with fat, its efficiency decreases. Fats and oils raise blood cholesterol, burdening the heart by causing atherosclerosis. Additionally, scientific evidence shows that fat prevents optimal sugar metabolism by cells and is the principal cause of adult-onset diabetes. Fat collects around cells and prevents glucose from getting beyond the cell membrane to the interior of the cells, where it would be transformed into fuel for cell metabolism. Excess fat, therefore, places a burden on the pancreas by reducing insulin efficiency. This makes the pancreas work harder to produce more insulin so that the cells have fuel.

I suggest that you check the face and other parts of the body to find out which meridians or diagnostic points are most affected by the fat and oil consumption. If the nose is oilier than the rest of the face, the heart is involved. If the forehead is oilier, the intestines and liver are the troubled organs. If the cheeks are oilier than the rest of the face, the lungs are burdened with too much fat. If the chin and mouth area is oilier, the sex organs and intestines are implicated.

ACNE

Pimples most often appear on the upper part of the body, especially on the face, shoulders, back, and chest. I believe pimples appear principally on the upper part of the body because pimples are a yin phenomenon. You will remember that the upper part of the body is yin; the lower is yang. Yin things expand and rise to the periphery. Yang things contract and descend to the center. Sugar and fat are yin. They all cause things to expand or grow. Everyone needs sugar, fat, and protein to live. But there are limits to our needs for these nutrients. When those limits are exceeded, the excess must be stored or gotten rid of. One of the ways for the body to eliminate excess is by pushing it out through the pores of the skin.

To treat acne, a person should avoid or eliminate all refined sugars and fatty foods. Under no circumstances should a person with acne eat so-called fast food, which is rich in fat and salt. This combination is extremely poisonous to the body because the salt causes the kidneys to contract, thus reducing their ability to filter the blood. When the kidneys cannot fully cleanse the blood, the toxins spread to tissues throughout the body and quickly become pimples. Remember that fat is difficult to digest because of its strong molecular bonds. Therefore, tiny globules of fat travel in the bloodstream. These globules are yin; they will rise in the body and finally emerge on the face or some other yin area of the skin, forming pimples.

When pimples appear on the face, you can use Oriental diagnosis to determine which organs and which meridians are most affected. Pimples on the cheeks indicate problems of the lungs; on the chin, of the sex organs; on the forehead, of the intestines and liver; on the nose, of the heart.

Pimples often appear from stress as well. Here again, the kidneys are involved. Stress directly affects the kidneys and kidney function, reducing their ability to filter blood.

A person who has acne should eat alkaline foods, chew well, get plenty of exercise to increase circulation and metabolism, and avoid excess sugar, fat, oils, and protein. Then acne is very easy to clear up.

ECZEMA

Eczema is a type of skin eruption, sometimes covering a large area of the skin. The skin becomes dry, flaky, and broken, and there may be mucus. Many people suffer from eczema and have great difficulty clearing it up. But like acne, eczema can be healed quickly and easily if only we live within our limits. The cause of eczema is in the elimination and circulation functions of the body.

If the amount of toxins we are taking in exceeds our body's ability to eliminate, there is a buildup in the blood. Additionally, circulation is poor, causing the toxins, especially fat and oil, to accumulate within the tissues below the surface of the skin. Antigens in the environment— anything from cat hair to pollen to air pollution—can trigger a reaction that is already waiting to take place. In this case, the antigen is like a fuse that sets off the dynamite already waiting to explode.

To cure eczema, we must seriously reduce or eliminate all refined sugars, fat, cholesterol, and refined foods, especially those with chemical additives. We must also reduce salt, which, if eaten excessively, will reduce kidney and bowel efficiency. This will cause toxins to accumulate in the bloodstream and result in further eczema.

DARK PATCHES AND FRECKLES

Dark patches, especially those that appear on the hands of older people, are caused by diminished efficiency of the liver. Brown patches occasionally appear on the hands along specific meridians, revealing that organs and related meridians are burdened. In general, brown patches are caused by excess fat and sugar consumption.

Freckles appear on the faces of children and are caused by excess consumption of fruit and sugar. Consumption of soda pop, candy, and other sweets is reduced as we grow older, and freckles gradually disappear. Although sunshine doesn't actually "cause" freckles, it is a trigger mechanism for people who are predisposed toward them.

DOUGHY SKIN

Often we see middle-aged and older people with doughy skin that is almost cheese-like. This is caused by the severe reduction of oxygen in particular tissues and organs. Note the places where these doughy deposits appear. I recommend that you use Oriental diagnosis to determine which organs and meridians are particularly involved.

THE HAIR

In Oriental diagnosis, hair outside the body has a direct and revealing relationship to hair inside the body, particularly the tiny hairs known as cilia that line the esophagus and digestive tract.

When a baby is inside its mother's womb for nine months, it is getting nourishment from the mother's blood. Therefore, the digestive tract is functionally dormant, though actively growing with the rest of the child. During those nine months, the child develops a soft, downy hair, called lanugo, that covers the body. Inside, tiny cilia are developing as well. Both the lanugo and the original cilia, however, are lost shortly after birth. The cilia are discharged along with the meconium, a mass in the child's bowel that contains amniotic fluids, dead cells, and lanugo swallowed by the child during gestation.

The elimination of cilia and outside hair occurs together. The baby sheds these hairs and then begins to develop a new, stronger, more resilient hair that will serve the inside and outside of the body. This is a healthy process, a growth step, for the child. He or she is adapting to the environment. The point here is that hair growth occurs naturally and in a coordinated fashion, so that hair inside and hair outside the body are always related.

In Oriental medicine, we believe that kidney, liver, and lung energy controls the growth and health of hair. The quality and quantity of our hair depend on our health. This is borne out by the fact that people who receive chemotherapy lose their hair. Chemotherapy, which is toxic to all cells, especially injures the kidneys. Once the kidneys are weakened, they are unable to provide adequate ki to the rest of the body, and those areas that are not essential to life—including the hair—are the last to be nourished. Consequently, the hair falls out.

Heavy metals and chemical poisons damage the liver and cause hair loss as well. These toxins are injurious to the liver and the kidneys, which have great difficulty cleansing them from the body. Consequently, they affect hair quality and growth.

Sea vegetables, especially the kelp family, can be instrumental in helping to eliminate chemical poisons and heavy metals. Research has demonstrated that sodium alginate—a constituent of most seaweeds— binds with heavy metals and chemical pollutants and leaches them from tissues. Once it binds with these toxins, it brings them into the intestines, where they can be eliminated from the body.

Emotional turmoil can cause hair to become thin, to fall out, or to change color. As pioneer researcher Hans Selye in Canada discovered recently, stress—or fear—injures the kidneys. Oriental medicine has been saying the same thing for three thousand years. Fear, the emotion associated with the kidneys, injures these most precious of organs. Negative emotions, such as sadness, anger, or fear, and chronic stress also harm the adrenal glands, which sit on the kidneys. The adrenals become hyperactive and overworked from long periods of stress, then ultimately they weaken and become underactive (hypoactive), further harming kidney energy. Therefore, emotional stress could cause hair loss by injuring the kidneys.

Kidney energy nourishes the sex organs. Hair—since it is governed by the kidneys—has always been associated in Oriental medicine with the sex organs. When you see a person's hair, you are getting an insight into the relative health and strength of his or her sex organs. Traditionally, women with beautiful, lustrous hair were seen as having the capacity to bear healthy children. With men, too, strong hair reflected strong liver, kidneys, and sex organs.

I find that people with split ends or brittle hair suffer from weak kidneys and sex organs. Split ends represent a yin condition—the hair divides at the end when it should remain contracted or unified. The cause is too much yin in the diet and life-style. The condition can also be caused by excessive use of drugs, either pharmaceuticals or recreational drugs. Brittle hair can come from consumption of too much salt or too much animal food; in either case, kidney energy is insufficient. Brittle hair can also be caused by an insufficiency of minerals, especially iodine. Increased consumption of land and sea vegetables can easily remedy this problem.

The condition of the outside hair also indicates the condition of the tiny hairs inside the body. Split ends or frizzy hair reveal the condition of the hair inside the lung and intestine as well. When hair appears later in life in places where it shouldn't, we know that something related to hair growth is occurring inside the body as well. For example, many women develop mustaches. The mouth area relates to the digestive tract and sex organs. Consequently, we know that there are excessive cilia in these areas of the body. The presence of excess cilia indicates that mucus accumulation has reached very high proportions. High levels of protein and mucus have resulted in increased hair growth within the digestive tract and sex organs. As more hair develops inside the body in these areas, more hair appears outside the body at specific diagnostic points. When a woman has a pronounced mustache, she likely suffers from problems related to the sex organs or menstrual cycle, including premenstrual syndrome and possibly fibroid cysts.

Whenever someone changes his or her dietary habits, I encourage careful attention to any alterations that affect the hair. Sometimes a diet can seem right intellectually but can be very wrong for us biologically. Our hair can tell us much about how our diet is affecting our lives.

BALDNESS

I believe that one of the causes of baldness is consumption of too much liquid. Each hair sits in a follicle, or bulb, which contains oil. When liquid consumption exceeds the kidneys' ability to process, the liquids cause the follicle bulb to expand, in turn causing the hair to fall out. People with thinning hair or baldness should consume less liquid and take excellent care of their kidneys.

Baldness usually occurs in specific sections of the head—either the front of the scalp or the back. If baldness appears in the front, the cause is excessive consumption of yin substances—especially soft drinks, fruit juices, and alcohol. If baldness appears in the back of the head or the center of the head, the cause is yang, that is, excessive consumption of salt, red meat, eggs, hard cheeses, and chicken.

Gray hair has long been associated with excess stress. It is common in the West to say, "I am going gray over this problem." As I have said, stress harms the kidneys and affects the hair. So, too, does excess salt, which causes the kidneys to contract and blocks the healthy flow of nutrients that would ordinarily go to the hair.

Men's facial hair can also be a sign of strength. Men with thick sideburns, for example, have strong livers and gallbladders. The gallbladder meridian runs along the back of the ear and side of the scalp, causing more lustrous and thicker hair to grow there. A strong mustache on a man can indicate natively strong digestive activity and sex organs.

In general, the growth of facial hair causes a man to become more yang, while shaving causes him to be more yin. Some men benefit in appearance from a beard, while others should never grow one. I think actor Kirk Douglas, for example, would look terrible with a beard because his face is so yang to begin with. His yang energy would be overwhelming and would ruin his appearance. On the other hand, Napoleon's face might have benefited from a beard, though Josephine didn't seem to mind it the way it was.

• • •

Hair and skin tell much about our health and our native strengths and weaknesses. But each can be improved dramatically by taking care of our daily lives, bodies, health, and especially of specific meridians. We should look to our bodies to find the secrets to our lives. Our bodies are constantly guiding us, offering us ways to turn our weaknesses into strengths and our unlovely parts into the natural beauty that exists within all of us.

that our philosophy included ... I respected his opinion, which was

A Program for Better Health

EATING FOR HEALTH AND HAPPINESS

It would be impossible to prescribe a specific diet that would be appropriate for everyone. Too often diets promote guilt and self-criticism. But the diet most people consume today is so unhealthful that virtually everyone can benefit by making some commonsense improvements.

Below are two sets of my general dietary guidelines. The first is a series of sensible recommendations designed to promote health, vitality, and long life.

The second set of guidelines is based on the Five Elements, or Five Transformations. Each element of the Five Transformations has a particular group of foods that enhance the function of the corresponding set of organs. If, after reading this book, you recognize that your spleen, liver, or kidney is not functioning well, you can begin eating more of the recommended foods for that particular element within the Five Transformations theory. This will enhance the functioning of the organs and related meridians to help restore health.

It is essential, however, that you eat a wide variety of foods. Don't misunderstand this advice to mean that you should concentrate exclusively on one particular element within the Five Transformations. All the organs in the body need to be nourished. For that to happen, you must eat a wide assortment of foods and enjoy many tastes. The advice provided below is a guideline for incorporating more of the foods that will help enhance the function of organs that currently may be functioning poorly. At the same time, it is important to seek out qualified health advice from a medical doctor or a holistic health counselor, or both.

GENERAL DIETARY GUIDELINES

1. *Be grateful for all the food that comes to you.* Food comes to us as a gift from the "Giver of Life." Receive it humbly and with gratitude. It is given to you to support your life here on this earth and to help you realize your most cherished dreams. Fortunately or unfortunately, I was born during World War II and was raised in Hiroshima prefecture, Japan. So I experienced from my stomach the truth of what I am saying. When you receive food, it comes to you with love, as a blessing from the world.

2. *Eat whole foods.* We humans are as much a product of nature as the stars and the trees and the plants. We are one with the soil: its minerals flow in our blood. We are one with the plants: their nutrients help our cells function and their fibers help us eliminate unwanted waste. We are one with the rain: our bodies are composed mostly of water. We are one with the sun: its rays give everything on the planet life.

Avoid food that has been stripped of its nutrient content or so heavily processed that it is more the product of the laboratory than of nature. Eat foods that are whole, fresh, unprocessed, and—whenever possible—organically grown. These foods will provide you with optimal amounts of nutrition and power. They will also help you avoid unwanted chemicals that lead to sickness and misery. They will lead you to live in harmony.

Especially eat whole grains, such as brown rice, millet, barley, oats, and corn; and fresh vegetables, particularly the leafy green variety, such as collards, kale, mustard greens, dark lettuce, and Chinese cabbage. Whole grains provide an abundance of energy—complex carbohydrates are the most efficient and powerful human fuel on the planet—as well as protein, vitamins, minerals, and fiber. Fresh vegetables are gold mines of vitamins, minerals, and fiber. These foods encourage the immune system and the elimination organs, and give us long-lasting energy.

3. *Chew your food well.* Chewing is an essential step in digestion. Humans are capable of eating anything, but first we must chew it. Food that is well chewed can be adequately digested and eliminated. Food that is only partially chewed cannot be fully digested. It causes all sorts of stomach and intestinal disorders and leads to sickness and unhappiness. Chew each mouthful thirty-five to fifty times for health, clear thinking, and happy digestion. Chewing well exercises the muscles in the mouth, jaw, and neck, which increases the blood supply to the brain, which needs thirty times more oxygen than the rest of your body. I believe that the more you chew the smarter you become.

4. *Avoid too much fat.* The most dangerous part of today's diet is fat. It is a proven carcinogen. It blocks oxygen and blood supply to tissues throughout the body. Without blood and oxygen, cells die. The body ages prematurely. Degenerative disease manifests. Excess consumption of fat causes cancer, heart disease, high blood pressure, adult-onset diabetes, premature senile dementia, and stroke. Animal foods, especially red meat, dairy products, and eggs, are loaded with fat. Eat these foods sparingly, if at all.

5. *Eat foods that are locally grown and in season.* We are living under specific climatic conditions, just as the plants that grow around us are. We should eat the foods that live under the same conditions we do. People who live in Alaska are better off eating fish and whale blubber than eating the foods and fruits of Brazil, and vice versa. It is the same with all other climates. When we eat the products of nature, we consume the energy that went into creating those plants. We are consuming our climate and all the energies that influence us each day. This makes it much easier for bodies to adjust to the seasons, the weather patterns, and the challenges we face in our daily lives. If you cannot eat locally grown foods, eat foods grown roughly on the same latitude as your own. Try to avoid foods that would not grow in your own climate.

6. *Do not overeat.* Overeating taxes the system, adds weight, and burdens digestion. It contributes to heart disease and intestinal and liver problems, and makes clear thinking difficult.

In Japan, we say that when the stomach is a little empty, the mind is hungry for knowledge. But when the stomach is full, the mind is full, too. I believe that if we ate less we would have fewer health problems.

7. *Do not eat just before sleeping.* It is a well-documented fact that during sleep the body is healing itself. This does not take place, however, if the stomach is full before bed. Energy that would be dedicated to healing goes instead to digestion. A full stomach prevents deep sleep and keeps us from getting adequate rest. A full stomach, I also think, causes us to dream excessively and makes our thoughts unhappy. This affects us the following day, making us lethargic and grumpy.

These are my suggestions for healthful eating. They are not too stringent. Anyone can follow them, and with much benefit.

DIET AND THE FIVE TRANSFORMATIONS

The Fire Element: The Heart and Small Intestine

The heart and small intestine are injured by too much spicy food, and by too much fat and cholesterol in the blood, caused by excessive consumption of animal foods. If a person's heart and small intestine are weak, he or she should reduce or eliminate from the diet red meat, eggs, and dairy food, all of which raise blood cholesterol and prevent the heart from receiving adequate blood and oxygen. The heart and small intestine are also weakened by overconsumption of foods that are too contracting or very cooling, such as salt.

Foods that enhance the fire element are corn, brussels sprouts, scallions, chives, red lentils, strawberries, and raspberries. Foods that are slightly bitter, such as dandelion greens, stimulate the heart and small intestine function.

Only small amounts of these foods are necessary, especially if they are eaten regularly (say, on a weekly basis). We should vary the assortment of fire foods. Reliance on any single group of foods will result in serious imbalances and eventually cause illness. We should remember to eat these foods in season; it is important to be in harmony with the environment and climate. Strawberries are not available in the winter for a reason—they are springtime fruits, meant to supplement the diet during a particular part of the year.

The heart and small intestine function are further enhanced by an optimistic attitude about life. Faith and gratitude stimulate joy.

The Earth Element: The Stomach and Spleen

Foods that harm the stomach and spleen are refined sugar and highly acidic foods. Highly sweetened drinks also injure the spleen.

Conversely, foods that have a mildly sweet taste enhance the spleen function. Squash and pumpkin are among the best spleen enhancers in the vegetable kingdom. Among grains, millet aids the spleen. People with stomach or spleen problems should eat plenty of millet and squash.

Minerals are very important to a well-functioning earth element. Since they contain minerals, all vegetables enhance the stomach, spleen, and pancreas function. Particularly helpful are collard greens, which are rich in minerals, especially calcium.

The earth element is further enhanced by chewing our food and salivating. Saliva can be highly alkaline, the stomach highly acidic. Well-chewed food, rich in saliva, goes into the stomach and buffers the stomach acids, making the stomach environment very harmonious. Spicy or acidic foods that are unchewed make the stomach environment highly acidic, causing heartburn, stomach discomfort, and, eventually, ulcers.

The Metal Element: The Lungs and Large Intestine

The metal element is enhanced by brown rice, and by many popular vegetables, including cabbage, cauliflower, celery, cucumber, watercress, turnips, radishes, and onions. According to Oriental medicine, gingerroot, daikon radish, garlic, and mustard greens are all medicinal herbs for the lungs and large intestine. Small amounts of pungent taste help improve lung and large intestine function as well.

Aerobic exercises, such as walking and bicycle riding, enhance both the lungs and large intestine. (See the section on meridian exercises later in this chapter.)

In general, fiber assists the whole intestinal tract by increasing transit time and moving old waste out of the system. Because they contain fiber, all whole grains and vegetables support and encourage the large-intestine function.

Conversely, animal foods, especially red meat, burden the intestines and make digestion more difficult. Fat, especially from red meat, eggs, and hard cheeses, is the number-one cause of colon cancer. Red meat is extremely hard to digest, especially since it cannot be fully masticated in the mouth and certainly cannot be broken down in the intestinal tract. People with large-intestine problems should avoid foods that are difficult to digest, especially meat.

The lungs are very sensitive to dairy products and oil. Fried foods, milk, yogurt, and other fatty or oily foods clog the tiny air sacs in the lungs, preventing full oxygenation of the lungs. If the lungs are to be healed, the diet must be low in oil and fat. If you cough, you should avoid bluefish, sardines, and mackerel.

The Water Element: The Kidneys and Bladder

Foods that enhance kidney function are beans and small amounts of salt. Too much salt, however, will weaken the kidneys and create high blood pressure; we should use small to moderate amounts of salt. All beans help to tone and enhance the kidney function, but adzuki beans are among the best.

Barley and buckwheat are the grains that best support the kidneys, while sea vegetables—especially kombu, hijiki, wakami, and nori—all serve to improve kidney function. When your kidney is tired, try gingerroot, which can be drunk as a tea, eaten as a vegetable, or applied as a compress.

The Wood Element: The Liver and Gallbladder

Excess greasy foods, fat, cholesterol, and alcohol injure the liver and gallbladder.

When a person has gallstones, he or she usually feels a stabbing pain in the lower chest area. Often the gallbladder is surgically removed, but gallstones can be gotten rid of naturally; they can be melted within the gallbladder by changing the diet to one that is considerably lower in fat and cholesterol. This lowers the cholesterol in the gallbladder, making the ratio between acid and cholesterol more balanced in favor of acid. To accomplish this, however, the person should be under the guidance of a skilled physician or nutritionist who can adjust the diet to lower the blood cholesterol level sufficiently without losing important nutrients. As long as the diet is dominated by whole grains, a wide variety of vegetables, beans, sea vegetables, and fish, there should be no problem getting all the nutrients needed for optimal health.

EXERCISES FOR HEALTH AND PEACE OF MIND

As I explained in chapter 3, the condition of our meridians directly affects our physical and psychological health. In a very practical way, we can see that the quality of our lives depends on the steady abundance of our energy. But we should be concerned not just with the quantity of our energy, but with how well it flows along certain meridian channels.

Emotional, dietary, and life-style patterns all affect the flow of energy in the body. We can correct imbalances and blockages of energy by changing our ways of eating and by doing meridian exercises regularly.

Below is a series of exercises designed to improve the flow of ki along specific meridians. These exercises, which I teach in my school, improve the function of the organs related to the meridians, as well as enhancing the emotional and psychological factors associated with each meridian. By doing these exercises, you will be able to diagnose the condition of your meridians. Stagnation of the flow along a specific meridian will show itself as stiffness or resistance to the exercise. Suppleness and flexibility reveal good ki flow and a well-functioning meridian.

Breathe deeply and steadily while doing each exercise. Try to remain balanced and relaxed. When you have reached the maximum stretching point for a specific exercise, hold that posture for a three-breath count, and then relax. Try to visualize and feel the energy flow along the meridians that you are exercising. Very important: do not push yourself too far beyond the point that your body is comfortable achieving. Do these exercises gently and purposefully. If you perform them regularly, you will quickly become more flexible and your health will improve noticeably. But be patient with yourself.

THE LUNG AND LARGE-INTESTINE MERIDIANS

Place your hands behind your back. Cross them, left hand above the right, and clasp them together with your thumbs. Bend forward while lifting your arms as high as possible. Hold this position, relax your muscles, and take two breaths. While you are holding the position, try to visualize ki rushing through your body from head to foot, especially through the shoulders, chest, and arms. You will likely feel some tension in your chest and shoulders and the backs of your legs. Relax completely. This exercise stretches the lung and large-intestine meridians. Do three or four repetitions, or as many as you can without straining.

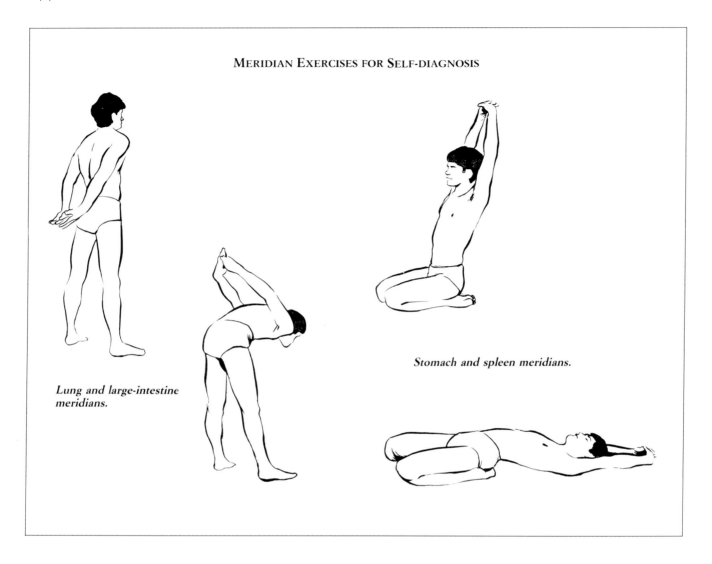

MERIDIAN EXERCISES FOR SELF-DIAGNOSIS

Lung and large-intestine meridians.

Stomach and spleen meridians.

THE STOMACH AND SPLEEN MERIDIANS

Kneel on the floor with your buttocks resting on your heels. Fold your hands together and lift them over your head as high as possible. Slowly allow your body to bend straight back until your back rests on the floor. Hold this position for two breaths and then return to your original position. You can also do this exercise with your palms facing toward the ceiling. This exercise is wonderful for the stomach and spleen meridians. Do three or four repetitions, or as many as you can without straining.

THE HEART AND SMALL-INTESTINE MERIDIANS

Sit on the floor. Place the soles of your feet together and bend and spread your knees to bring your feet as close to your body as possible.

MERIDIAN EXERCISES FOR SELF-DIAGNOSIS

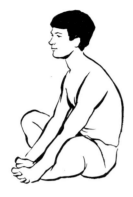

Kidney and bladder meridians.

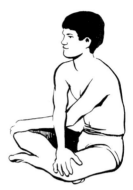

Heart and small-intestine meridians.

Heart constrictor and triple heater meridians.

Liver and gallbladder meridians.

Hold your feet with your hands. Place your elbows on your knees and try to touch your head to your toes. At the same time, try to have your knees touch the floor. Ideally, you should be able to touch your head to your toes while your knees touch the floor. Do not strain. Reach your maximum stretching point and hold that posture for two breaths. Relax. Inability to touch your head to your toes while your knees touch the floor indicates problems in the heart and small intestine. Regular use of this exercise will improve the function of both organs.

THE KIDNEY AND BLADDER MERIDIANS

While sitting on the floor, stretch your legs straight out and touch your toes with your hands. At the maximum stretching point, hold the position, relax your muscles, and take two breaths. Feel the ki flow through your body, especially along your back and legs.

THE HEART CONSTRICTOR AND TRIPLE HEATER MERIDIANS

Sit in the lotus position or half lotus (with the sides of your feet resting on the floor, rather than the more difficult posture that places your feet on the inside of your legs). Cross your arms and take hold of the opposite knee with each hand. Bend forward and rest your head on the floor. While holding this position, relax all your muscles, visualize the ki flowing through your body, especially in the back of your upper body and arms, and take two deep breaths.

THE LIVER AND GALLBLADDER MERIDIANS

Sit on the floor. Stretch your legs out straight to the side, as wide apart as possible. Fold your hands together and stretch your arms over your head, then bend to the side and try to touch your toes with the insides of your hands. At the maximum stretching point, relax, take two deep breaths, and resume a normal posture. This exercise stretches the liver and gallbladder meridians.

Regular use of these exercises will make your body strong yet flexible, and will enable you to evaluate your own condition. You will develop excellent muscle tone because ki will flow in greater abundance throughout your body. Yoga philosophy has long maintained that flexibility of body is reflected in flexibility of mind and spiritual outlook. Resistance in the body reflects stubborn attitudes about life. As you perform these exercises regularly, you will notice not only greater vitality and flexibility, but also clearer thinking and more creativity. As your body becomes more flexible, so too will your mind. Where once you believed a particular problem was unsolvable, suddenly you will realize new possibilities inherent in the situation. You will begin to feel a greater sense of opportunity when you face challenges. In short, as you become stronger and more flexible, your life will seem more manageable.

A Sample Diagnosis
and Conclusion

As an exercise, let me share a recent Ohashiatsu session so that you can see, at least to some extent, how you can apply the knowledge I have discussed to a living, breathing human being.

Most of the time, my clients come to my school in Manhattan. Today I am scheduled to see a man I will call Mr. Robert Smith. I have never met him. I do not know why he has come to me.

When he arrives, he enters the foyer and is asked by my receptionist to take off his shoes. The receptionist then pages me to let me know Mr. Smith has arrived. I greet him in my normal, friendly way, grasping his thick, strong hand and bowing, as is my custom.

"How do you do, Mr. Smith!" I say. "It's so good to see you. Please come in, please come in."

With that, I escort him to my big Japanese room, where I offer him tea. He examines the small porcelain teacup for a moment and then begins to drink the tea.

"What kind of tea is this?" he asks me.

"This is Japanese tea," I say. "Very good tea we have."

"Very tasteful tea," he says.

He takes a moment to taste the tea. He has a sensitive tongue. I note his awareness. It is a good sign, a sign of good stomach and heart and appreciation. He is open. Already, I am optimistic about his ability to overcome any problem he has, no matter what it is.

I begin by engaging him in some friendly discussion. I ask him how he arrived—by cab or by subway? "Car," he says. He's probably not a New Yorker.

"Where are you from?" I ask.

"Westfield, New Jersey," he says.

We discuss the traffic, the weather, and how he likes visiting New York.

As he speaks, I examine him closely as I am listening. He is in his fifties. His head is a vertical rectangle, with a square jaw and an equally square forehead. There are three complete zones on his face—the forehead, cheekbones, and chin are all about the same size—making his head longer than it is wide. His eyes are small, round, and open. Between them are two shallow vertical lines. Below each eye is a small, slightly swollen eye bag; however, the bags are not very pronounced.

His nose is of medium length, with a swollen bulb at the end. The surface of his nose is slightly bumpy.

His cheeks are tight and lightly lined. His mouth shows little or no lip. When he closes his mouth, it closes tight, becoming a horizontal line. Shallow vertical lines run from each nostril to the corners of his mouth. Overall, his face is whitish to pale in color. The face is tight and strong, but it looks slightly swollen.

His ears are medium in size, and thick. Their most noticeable characteristic is a well-developed rim around the edge. The inner line that runs from the ear hole to the outer rim is not well developed. The upper ridge, inside the ear, is strong, and there is a small channel passing through the upper ridge within the ear. The earlobe is full and strong, but it is attached to the side of the head, as opposed to hanging free.

Mr. Smith has light brown markings on his cheeks and forehead. His hair is light brown, but with traces of gray. His hairline has receded along the sides of his head, so that the foresection of the hairline comes forward, while the sides retreat in long loops.

His arms are muscular, with thick wrists. His hands are wide and strong, his fingers wide, stubby, and medium in length. His fingernails are short. He is about five feet, ten inches tall, of medium build, and looks fit, especially for a man in his fifties. He has a slight paunch. Overall, he has the body of a former athlete that has now become hard with stagnation. I can sense his stiffness.

He has a direct look, and his head turns downward slightly at the end of his sentences, so that his chin tucks toward his chest to emphasize a point.

"How long have you lived in New Jersey?" I ask.

"Twenty years," he tells me.

"Before that? Where did you grow up?"

"California," he says. He then proceeds to tell me a few polite things about where he grew up in California.

As he talks, I let Mr. Smith's energy wash over me. I am completely open; I have no resistance, none whatsoever. I am without mind, empty of all thoughts. The air between us now is charged with his energy alone. I feel this man's life. It fills my every pore. His presence is like a book that is being read to me. I am being bombarded by the information that emanates from this man. My job is to take it in without reflection and let my unconscious sort it out and feed it back to my conscious mind.

Mr. Smith punctuates much of what he says with a little smile. That is revealing—an optimistic man. He smiles often, but I also sense a yearning in his smile, almost a sadness. Perhaps he hasn't achieved the success he wanted, or thinks he should have had. There is both a sadness and a compassion in his voice and his face.

At the same time, there is considerable strength and directness in his manner. He is not broken. he has lived and suffered, but his dream is alive. That I can feel in the little smile and the brightness and openness in his eyes. He hasn't given up. What a victory! I think to myself. A man who has lived, struggled, failed and succeeded, and still believes in the goodness of life—a man who still believes in the future!

Even before I ask him why he has come to see me, I know many of Mr. Smith's problems and strengths.

He is rigid. His body is stiff. So, too, is his manner. This means that he is a conventional thinker, and one who suffers a lot of frustration because he lacks the capacity to bend in adversity. He will endure, but painfully.

He has heart disease, as indicated by the swollen nose and bumpy skin on the bulb of his nose. The cause of his problem is the consumption of too much animal food, or too much fat and not enough vegetables. His heart is suffocating from lack of oxygen. There is simply too much fat around his heart and too much cholesterol plaque in the arteries leading to the heart. He's on his way to a heart attack or stroke. His face is also slightly swollen, further indicating a heart condition.

He also has severe digestive problems, as indicatd by the fact that his mouth shows little or no lip. The blotches on his forehead indicate some stagnation in his intestinal tract; he probably carries much un-eliminated waste. More than likely, he suffers from chronic diarrhea. His small and large intestine are suffering badly and probably degenerating, as indicated by the lines running from his nose to his mouth. Also, the inner ridge of his ear, which indicates the constitutional strength of his intestines, is faint. He was not born with strong intestines. This is his weak point, but he hasn't lived according to his weakness. He has a passion for steak and other animal foods. If he doesn't change soon, he will suffer from some type of serious intestinal disease—colon cancer, perhaps. The stagnation in his intestines and elsewhere is also the central cause of his rigidity.

Since digestion is also intimately connected with the spleen, I know that his spleen is weak too. Probably he has some stomach trouble: chronic heartburn, acidity, or an ulcer.

His kidneys are overworked and tired (as indicated by the slight eye bags), but still strong. Constitutionally, he has strong kidneys, as revealed by his strong, thick ears.

He may have been a drinker once, but I sense that he no longer imbibes alcohol. I see this in several signs. His face is white. If he were still a problem drinker his face would be red, the result of many swollen capillaries around his nose, eyes, and cheeks. The swelling of the capillaries is caused by the yin, or expansive, effect of the alcohol. Also, his face is relatively clear and tight; there isn't a lot of liquid in his face. His eyes are essentially clear, also.

The whiteness of his skin tells me that his lungs and large intestine are troubled. Since he definitely has intestinal disease, the lungs will naturally be troubled as well.

Perhaps he had a drinking problem and has since given up alcohol. That may be the source of some sad memories, as well as the reason that he may have a marked degree of frustration over how far he has gone in his work or career. (I will say nothing about this, unless he asks my opinion.)

Mr. Smith's voice reveals a touch of grief or sadness, despite his smile. Again, that indicates the intestinal problem and some bad memories. He's wearing a ring on his fourth finger. Perhaps he and his family have been able to come through a turbulent emotional period. Judging by his optimistic expression and his strengths, I believe he has.

His liver has been stressed, but is still strong. The two vertical lines between his eyes indicate a problem with the liver. Again, I note the possible problem with alcohol. But since the lines are not especially deep, and there are two, rather than just one deep one, his liver is not as troubled as it might be. It suffers from congestion, again from the consumption of too much animal food—especially meat and hard cheese.

He has no discernible anger in his voice, indicating that the liver may not be acutely troubled at this moment.

His right shoulder is slightly higher than his left. This tells me that his liver and ascending colon are swollen, while his spleen and descending colon are contracted. His right leg will be longer than his left, causing shoulder pain and some distortion in his spine. He probably has pain in the middle of his back. He will need plenty of Ohashiatsu and a change in life-style (including diet) if he is to correct this structural imbalance.

The dark patches on his face indicate stagnation in the intestines and lungs (the cheeks reveal the condition of the lungs). Dark patches also reveal the consumption in the past of too much sugar. Current problems with sugar consumption are revealed by redness (swollen capillaries), but if one has had a history of excess sugar intake and has since given it up, that is often revealed as dark patches on the face. Redness indicates a current problem with strong yin substances, such as sugar, sweeteners, fruit and fruit juice, and alcohol. Dark patches also indicate liver problems. The liver is no longer able to fully cleanse the blood of fats and sugars, causing many of these carbohydrates to build up within the liver and eventually to be discharged in the form of carbon, or dark patches along certain meridian lines.

Despite these obvious problems, I am deeply impressed by Mr. Smith's inherent strengths and the overwhelming goodness that seems to radiate from him. To begin with, he is possessed of a strong constitution, as suggested by his well-proportioned, squarish head. The three zones of his face are all well developed, indicating a strong intellect, emotional nature, and will. His thick ears and ample earlobes reveal strong kidneys and a man well endowed with character, breadth of vision, and understanding of life.

His philtrum is also strong and pronounced, suggesting a strong will, commitment, and sexual vitality. His strong constitution suggests that he has an excellent chance of recovering his health.

As for his character, I see that he is dedicated and a hard worker. He's not a visionary or a revolutionary—those characteristics would be revealed in a more yin-shaped head and larger eyes (witness the faces of Gandhi and Lenin)—but he has the capacity to see far and think things through, as indicated by the high forehead.

His eyes are small. This indicates a strong attention to detail. He can work with numbers, mechanical tools, and mathematical formulas. His hands and fingers are stubby, further suggesting a man who is practical in nature, one who enjoys working with his hands on hard problems. He's tough and enduring, though his resilience is weakening now because of his rigidity and conventional thinking. He will follow regulations to a fault and will resist breaking free of organizations and institutions. He'll stick to the tried and true.

He could be an engineer, a scientist, a builder, or a computer programmer. He's a team player, a leader within his institution.

This type of man has great difficulty when he becomes too yang, which almost always happens to people with his type of constitution. They are so preoccupied with details and the conventional approach that they fail to look up at the sky. They forget that the order of the universe has everything in hand. Instead, such people take on too much responsibility for the way things develop, causing them frustration and an overwhelming sense that things are out of control. They forget that they are riding the order of the universe, not directing the universe itself.

Yet Mr. Smith is not without a strong spiritual nature. Indeed, I sense, by his open eyes and face and his little smile, that faith has won out after all. He may have surrendered to God, or is now in the process of doing so.

"What can I do for you?" I ask Mr. Smith.

"Well, I have several nagging problems. I've been to doctors and am taking medication but nothing seems to be working. I'm afraid that if I do not do more than take drugs, I'll just get worse."

From there, Mr. Smith tells me that he has numerous digestive problems and that he's recently been diagnosed as having heart disease. The medication he is taking for both problems is making him feel worse. A mutual friend has suggested that he see me. He is hoping that I may be able to help him.

"What do you do for a living?" I ask.

"I work for IBM in a management position," he says. He was formerly a computer programmer but was elevated to management.

"Are there any symptoms? Any pain or discomfort?" I ask.

"I have a lot of stomach gas, and sometimes heartburn," he says. "Also, I go back and forth from diarrhea to constipation."

"Which one do you suffer from most—diarrhea or constipation?" I ask.

"Diarrhea," he says. "I also have angina that comes when I stress my heart or when it's too cold outside. Then I get the pain."

"Please stand up," I ask him. "You see that your right shoulder is higher than your left?

"I do now. I never really noticed."

"Most people don't notice, so don't feel bad," I say. "That means that one leg is shorter than the other, too. Also, one side of your body is too tight, too tense, the other side too loose and expanded. This means left-right imbalance.

"Do you have any back pain?" I ask. I put my hand on the middle of his back and say, "Maybe right here."

"Sometimes, especially when I'm sitting for a while," Mr. Smith says.

"I am not a doctor and I do not prescribe medicine," I say. "I can give you regular Ohashiatsu, which can help you with your physical imbalances. You should also consider changing your way of eating. I can give you a general dietary plan that can help you with these problems and also ask you to eat specific foods that can assist your digestion, and I want to describe specific exercises for you to practice every day."

I explain my ideas. In a very slow and patient manner, I explain that he's too yang—too contracted, especially in the coronary arteries and the intestines. The accumulation of fat and cholesterol has narrowed the arteries and the intestinal tract; it has also weakened the intestines' ability to absorb nutrients and move waste out of the body.

Mr. Smith's kidneys and lungs are also troubled. There are more toxins in the blood than those organs can eliminate. Consequently, much remains behind, in both the blood and the organs themselves.

I must make him more relaxed. To do this, he needs regular Ohashiatsu; exercise; and a change in diet to include more grains, vegetables, and beans and less animal food, especially meat, eggs, and hard cheeses. The exercise can be simple. It must, however, be done regularly.

"Are you willing to make adjustments in your life-style, such as dietary change, some mild form of exercise, and regular Ohashiatsu?" I ask.

"That's why I'm here," Mr. Smith says with a smile.

"Good. You continue to work with your doctor, and I will do as much for you as I can with Oriental diagnosis."

Then we go into the next room and we begin with Ohashiatsu.

CONCLUSION

I began this book by saying that you are perfect the way you are and fully capable of being happy. Perhaps, after reading this book, you may feel that many things are wrong with your physiognomy. Let me repeat myself: there is nothing wrong with you! Everything about you is right.

Life is made possible by paradox. Peace is attained by the joining of opposites. Each of us has strengths and weaknesses. The key to happiness is self-knowledge and self-realization. I have tried to help you understand yourself better by revealing your inner nature through the use of the Oriental diagnosis which I have developed.

Oriental diagnosis teaches us that if we have weak kidneys, it is unwise to live as if we have strong kidneys. That will only make us unhappy. In other words, we are perfect as we are, but we must live according to our unique perfection. We must be who we are.

Everyone has strengths and weaknesses. This is the very combination that makes us unique and gives us direction in life. Look at my picture on the jacket of this book. Now that you know Oriental diagnosis, you can see many imperfections in Ohashi's face. Look at all the wonderful imperfections that make up Ohashi. Each of them is proof of my uniqueness. I am so fortunate. I have a place in life that no one else has.

The secret to happiness is to know your weaknesses, know your strengths, and live accordingly. Take care of your weaknesses and use your strengths.

"Follow your bliss," said the great mythologist Joseph Campbell. In this book, I want to say the same thing. Through self-knowledge you discover where your talents lie; you discover your weaknesses, too. You discover those things that do not support your life. At that point, you can do what you love to do, and avoid the abuse of your weaknesses. In this way, you will avoid much pain, suffering, and confusion.

Once you've made those discoveries, you are enlightened. All there is left to do is to live a happy life.

Index

Page numbers in *italics* refer to illustrations.